IMAGES
of America

CLARKSBURG

This statue of Gen. Thomas J. Stonewall Jackson, who was born in Clarksburg, Virginia, in 1824, has for years stood on the Harrison County Courthouse Plaza in downtown Clarksburg, West Virginia.

IMAGES
of *America*

CLARKSBURG

Robert F. Stealey

ARCADIA
PUBLISHING

Published by Arcadia Publishing
Charleston, South Carolina

Library of Congress Catalog Card Number: 2005920051

For all general information contact Arcadia Publishing at:
Telephone 843-853-2070
Fax 843-853-0044
E-mail sales@arcadiapublishing.com
For customer service and orders:
Toll-Free 1-888-313-2665

Visit us on the Internet at www.arcadiapublishing.com

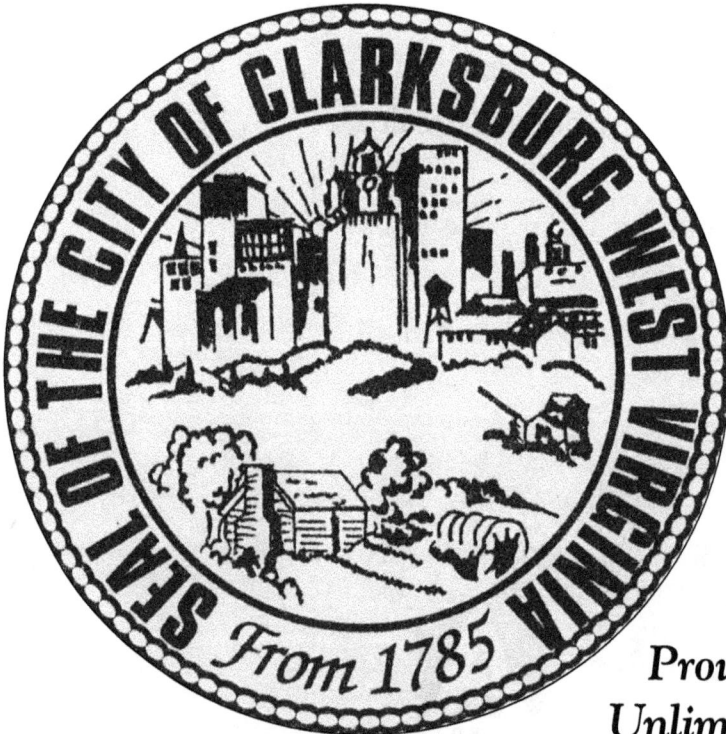

Proud Past . . .
Unlimited Future!

CONTENTS

ACKNOWLEDGMENTS

Numerous are the sources that have made Images of America: *Clarksburg* a reality. Perhaps foremost is the Harrison County Historical Society, whose president, Cris Green, has entrusted me with an abundance of photographs. Also, Dick Duez of nearby Bridgeport has made available quite a few images that have never been published prior to now. Ronnie Smith of Clarksburg was also a contributor of some mid-20th century images.

Further, I have been able to use a number of photographs from my own collection, many of which I once never considered would be appearing in book form.

In addition, I would like to acknowledge the City of Clarksburg, West Virginia, for lending to me documents dating back to the early 20th century; the Clarksburg Fire Department, for some of its photos of major blazes that its members have battled through the years; and the Clarksburg Police Department for its share of pictures.

For the text in this work, I excerpted a large amount of information from *A History of Harrison County*, by the late Dorothy Davis, which was copyrighted in 1970 by the American Association of University Women and published by McClain Printing Company of Parsons, West Virginia. I received invaluable assistance from David Houchin of the Clarksburg-Harrison Public Library and Mrs. Cecil B. Highland Jr.

There are others, too numerous to mention, who produced material for me to include in the following pages. And I'd be remiss were I not to mention my editor, Lauren Bobier of Arcadia Publishing, whose accommodating spirit and patience I shall never forget.

Finally, I'd like to thank my wife, Nadine, who overlooked the images and the notebooks in which I recorded my work scattered on a large portion of the living room floor.

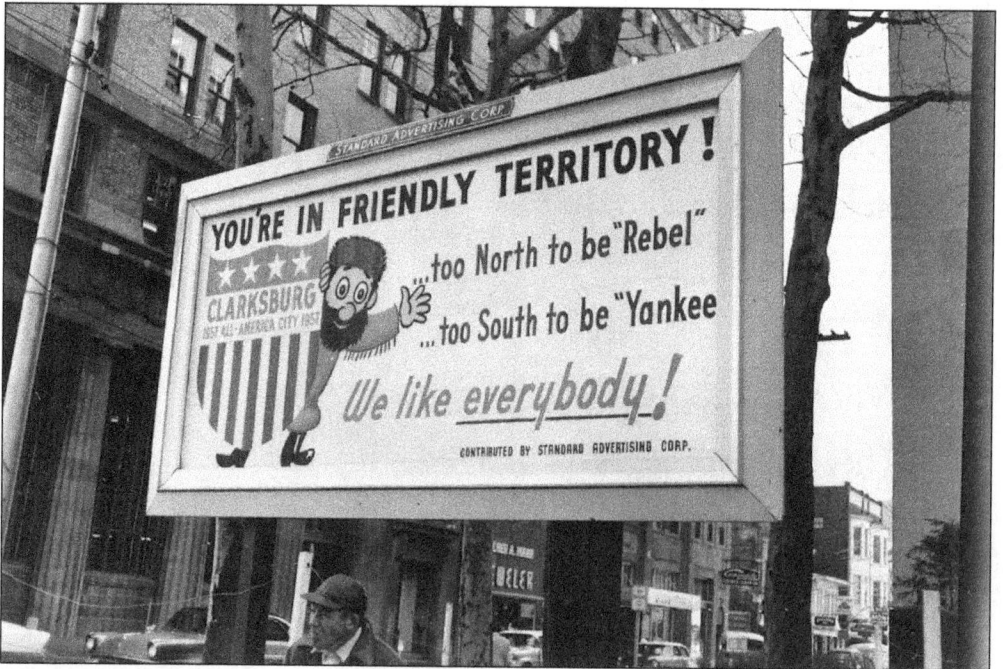

This friendly billboard greeting to Clarksburg residents and visitors once stood just behind the wall of the Harrison County Courthouse on West Main Street.

INTRODUCTION

Many of the sights of Clarksburg that are included in this work are quite vivid in my memory, while others are from the many years before I arrived in the city from Australia, my birthplace, at the young age of six months.

The more than 200 images in this, my third book for Arcadia, perhaps go more to provide a feel for the familiar locations and landmarks found in Clarksburg than to submit a mini-history of the city named for Revolutionary War colonel George Rogers Clark and the birthplace of Confederate general Thomas Jonathan "Stonewall" Jackson, who fought in the War Between the States.

This author wishes that the following chapters would have included many more images of Clarksburg, which has been dubbed by some "Jewel of the Hills." However, it is hoped that the memories herein will spur many a conversation among families and friends, either current or former residents of Clarksburg.

The city with an elevation of 1,400 feet above sea level is surrounded by hills, especially to the north and south. Pinnickinnick Hill, which was named by Native Americans who are a part of Clarksburg's history, rises to the north, while Lowndes Hill is to the south.

In the early and middle 20th century, Clarksburg was quite the hub of central West Virginia, as was evidenced by the number of shoppers on the sidewalks of the city's central business district, better known as "downtown." The census of the city in 1950 was 32,014, and it was the fourth largest in West Virginia, exceeded only by Charleston, Huntington, and Wheeling.

Today, Clarksburg has followed the trend of many other American cities of its size. It has seen a loss of industry and a movement of business from the mid-city to the outlying areas. Eastpointe and New Pointe shopping centers to the east have the greatest concentration of retail business in the area. People from Clarksburg and many other communities in the north-central region of the state visit the Super Wal-Mart, one of the largest of that chain east of the Mississippi River. The Meadowbrook Mall in nearby Bridgeport also attracts a number of shoppers from Clarksburg.

Today, the West Virginia Italian Heritage Festival, the Black Heritage Festival, and the Ethnic Festival call Clarksburg home. Numerous parades take place through the streets of downtown Clarksburg, including the annual Greater Clarksburg Associates Christmas Parade, the Veterans Day Parade, and the Italian Heritage Festival Parade.

Clarksburg has its share of parks and playgrounds, too. Clarksburg City Park is located to the south in nearby Nutter Fort and features playground facilities for children, a picnic area with shelters under shade trees, a miniature golf course, a basketball court, and several baseball fields, including Frank Loria Memorial Field, which has hosted many high school, American Legion, and Babe Ruth League tournaments.

There are three high schools in Clarksburg—Robert C. Byrd High School, Liberty High School, and Notre Dame High School—where fans can catch football, basketball, baseball, and soccer games in season.

One of the largest hospitals in West Virginia, the United Hospital Center, is located in Clarksburg. Also, the Louis A. Johnson Veterans Administration Medical Hospital has been in Clarksburg for more than half a century.

For you readers who wish to look back with fondness on a place you have called home, here's hoping the images that follow will evoke many pleasant memories for you.

—Robert F. Stealey

A symbol of the Ten Commandments stood just outside the front door of the Harrison County Courthouse. Clarksburg is the Harrison County seat.

One

EARLY TIMES

The seat of Harrison County government is Clarksburg, where the courthouse on West Main Street at the corner of South Third Street is considered by many to be the center of town. A small statue of native son Stonewall Jackson stands on the Harrison County Courthouse Plaza. On the next few pages are views of Clarksburg as it appeared in the 19th and early 20th centuries. Some of its former landmarks, such as the Trader's Hotel, are only memories today. At one time, some of the sections of Clarksburg such as North View, Adamston, and Stealey were incorporated towns themselves. Residents of Clarksburg today have only the stories passed down from previous generations and the countless pages of local history books to learn much about the city's very early times. It's good to know, though, that earlier days in Clarksburg are represented in the city's new motto, "Proud Past. . . Unlimited Future!"

Birthplace of Stonewall Jackson, Clarksburg, W. Va.

This picture postcard shows an illustration of the birth of Clarksburg's favorite son, Stonewall Jackson, with an inset of his statue. A plaque appears today at the site of his birth, 330 West Main Street downtown.

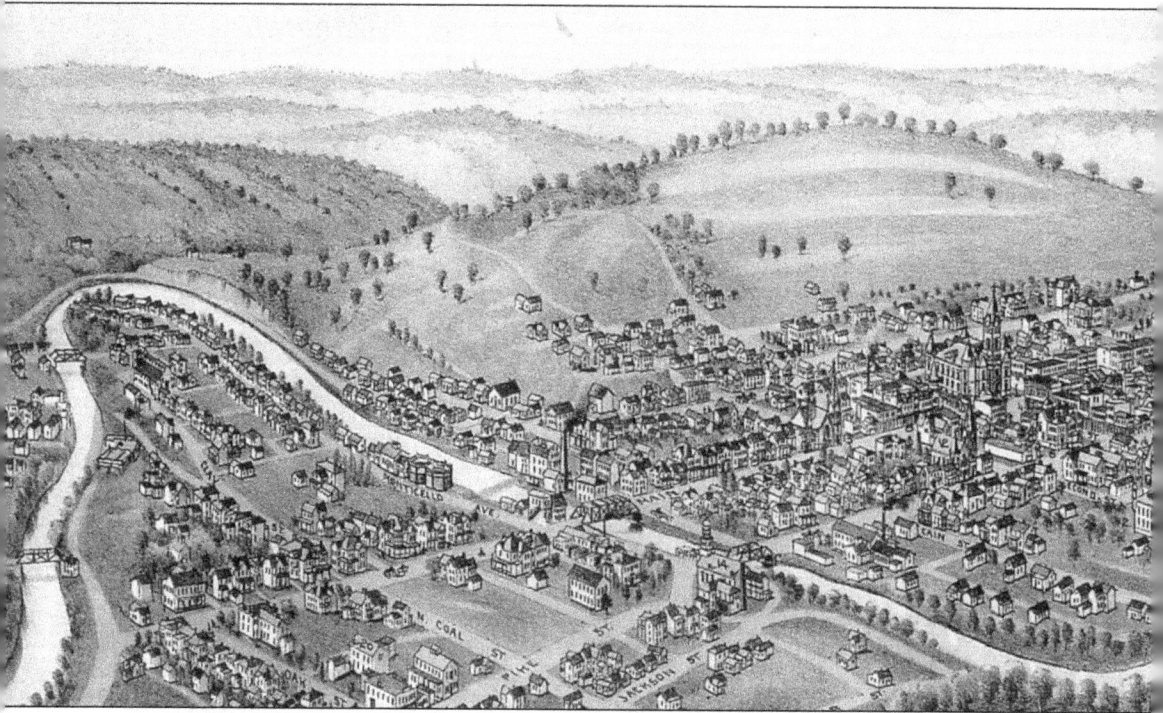

T.M. Fowler of Morrisville, Pennsylvania, produced this illustration of Clarksburg as it appeared in 1898. His original illustration also included images of dominant Clarksburg

Pike Street in 1910 had a brick surface with a streetcar track down the middle that remained for years. This appears to be the current 300 block of West Pike in downtown Clarksburg. (Courtesy of Dick Duez.)

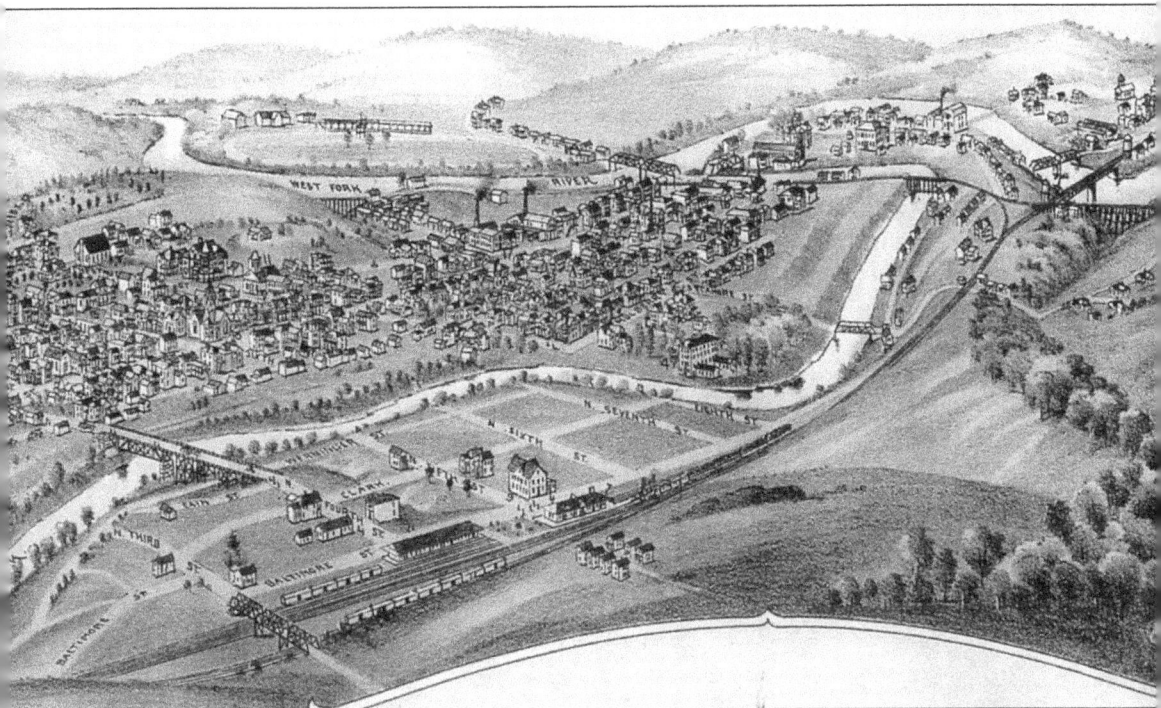

landmarks. The names of major streets, some of which have since changed, are shown. (Courtesy of Mike Angiulli.)

The Lowndes and Chorpening Mill was located along the Elk Creek. Ownership of the mill changed many times. The Clarksburg Automobile Company was the last owner, and the mill was demolished in 1929. (Courtesy of Cris Green, Harrison County Historical Society president.)

The unveiling of the Soldier's Monument took place May 30, 1908, in what was then known as the "courthouse yard" in Clarksburg. The horse and small runabout, in foreground, belonged to C.O. Findley. Mr. and Mrs. C.O. Findley are in the runabout, and "Dominion Maud" is in the harness. (Courtesy of Cris Green, Harrison County Historical Society president.)

The Citizens Bakery of Clarksburg was located in Glen Elk No. 2, near the brick factory. The individuals shown were not identified. (Courtesy of Dick Duez.)

Taken from near the intersection of Pike and Second Streets, this photo shows the HC Sinclair service station at right foreground and the Enraw Building in background. The street lamps of old have recently made a comeback as part of the city's restoration project. (Courtesy of Ronnie Smith.)

A Stonewall Jackson celebration was held in 1957. Those with roles in the event were Adam Skasik, left, and Luther Williams. (Courtesy of Anna Walsh.)

These gentlemen, portrayers in the Stonewall Jackson celebration of 1957 in Clarksburg, ride a buckboard in front of a local residence. From left to right are (in front) Adam Skasik and Luther Williams; (in back) Dave Hostutler and Marty Williams.

This building appears to be fronted by a cornfield. It was known as the Northwestern Hotel, later the Walker House, and was across Pike Street from where the Hotel Gore stands today. It was run by James Carder in the middle of the 19th century. (Courtesy of Cris Green, Harrison County Historical Society president.)

The Tuna Hotel in Clarksburg, of which P.M. Gary was proprietor, was believed to be located in the city's Industrial section on Tuna Street, which is known as Broadway today. (Courtesy of Cris Green, Harrison County Historical Society president.)

Orie Myers is at the reins of this carriage outside his hardware store, which was located on Hewes Avenue in Clarksburg. In addition to hardware, the firm also dealt in feed and vehicles. His son, Paul Myers, took over ownership and moved the business to 434 West Pike Street near the VFW building. The business was later demolished. (Courtesy of Dick Duez.)

Shadowed by an awning one sunny day in 1961, this is the plaque at 330 West Main Street in downtown Clarksburg that marks the birthplace of Gen. Thomas Stonewall Jackson.

Two

PUBLIC AND
PRIVATE BUSINESS

When Americans refer to business today, it is often in two categories—public and private. Public pertains to transactions in federal, state, or local government, while private deals with profit-making entities such as big and small business. Clarksburg is, by virtue of its charter, a strong city manager form of government. Its city council consists of seven members, one of whom is mayor and another is vice-mayor. City elections are held every two years, in the "off-years," when national and state elections are not held. City business is centered in the new Clarksburg Municipal Building, located catty-corner to the Harrison County Courthouse downtown. Private business involves manufacturing, retail sales, and profit-making corporations or businesses. Both are represented by images on the following pages.

This group of young fellows wearing coats and ties poses for a photo while standing on the War Memorial in the courthouse yard in downtown Clarksburg. The picture was taken in 1911. In the background is the Merchants Bank Building, which today houses the People's Bank, and at right is the R.T. Lowndes Department Store, the site on which the Clarksburg Municipal Building stands today. (Courtesy of Dick Duez.)

ADMINISTRATION AND FINANCE

"Administration and finance" include the activities of the city council, the city manager, the city clerk, the city attorney, the city treasurer, the operation of the city building, conducting of city elections and other functions usually classed as "general government."

Under our present charter the expiration of the two-year term of city councilmen does not coincide with the end of the fiscal year. Thus one council served ten months of the past year, while the present council, coming into office May 1st, held the reins for the last two months. Five members of the new council were also members of the old. The administrative branch of government remained practically unchanged.

During the year, the council:

Held 42 meetings;
Enacted 77 ordinances;
Passed 702 resolutions;
Approved payment 1327 bills;
Granted 595 building permits;
Approved issuing 725 licenses;
Ordered 468 sidewalks built;
Received hundreds of reports;
Heard scores of petitions;
And transacted other business.

Everybody Kept Busy

The street improvement schedule involving 80 separate projects kept all administrative officials on the jump. Seventy-three ordinances and fully two-thirds of the resolutions of the council dealt with these improvements. Over half the time of the manager, attorney, clerk and treasurer and most of the efforts of the engineer's office were devoted to this work. It was the biggest paving year in the city's history, yet other activities have kept pace to make a well rounded program.

New Seal an Inspiration

Pioneer spirit, natural resources, industry, commerce, progress and prosperity at the dawn of the new day are all symbolized in Clarksburg's new city seal.

Designed by Virginia M. Wood.

CLARKSBURG'S CITY FLAG

"A bright red, five-pointed star, symbolizing the city of Clarksburg, composed of five former towns—served by two intersecting state highways, represented by white bars extending diagonally corner to corner, across a bright blue field,—the bars radiating to the four corners of the flag being likewise symbolic of Clarksburg products distributed to the four corners of the earth,—a further symbolism denoting the star of hope with the sky as the limit,—the colors red, white and blue, being suggestive of the national flag, as allegiance to the City of Clarksburg implies a greater allegiance to the nation."—Council Records.

Illustrations of Clarksburg's flag and seal appear on this page of the Second Annual Report of the City Manager to the City Council in 1923. (Courtesy of the City of Clarksburg.)

The Clarksburg
TOWN CRIER

By Authority of the City Government
For the Benefit of the Citizens of the Good City of Clarksburg

VOLUME I, NO. 7   CLARKSBURG, WEST VIRGINIA   JULY, 1923

City Publishes The Town Crier

Sixty-five Hundred Copies Mailed Each Issue Without Charge to Clarksburg Homes.

In January, 1923, by authorization of the city council, the administration published the first issue of the Clarksburg Town Crier. Its pages are devoted to stories of city activities, discussion of public problems and departmental news items. The cost of publication is covered by receipts from advertising.

Some 6,500 copies are mailed without charge to Clarksburg homes each issue. An important feature of nearly every number is the information and complaint directory. This directory lists alphabetically all the city activities of general interest and gives the telephone number and name of the city employe to be called.

Thru the columns of the Town Crier, was conducted the contest for designs for the new city seal and the city flag. One issue featured a map of the city. Judging from the many comments heard, from complaints when an issue is late, and from the steady advertising support, the efforts required have been quite worth while.

Parents are reporting diseases more promptly. Merchants are instructing their janitors to put sidewalk sweepings into the trash can instead of the gutter. Housewives with complaints are calling up the right offices. Curbstone criticism, based on lack of information, is less common. Understanding of what the city administration is for, what it is doing and what it hopes to do, is more general. Community consciousness and team work seem to be increasing. All of which are good signs and in keeping with the purpose of the Town Crier.

7

Here's the first page of *The Clarksburg Town Crier*, a 1923 newsletter that was mailed to Clarksburg homes free of charge "for the benefit of the citizens of the good city of Clarksburg." (Courtesy of the City of Clarksburg.)

SECOND ANNUAL REPORT
OF THE CITY MANAGER TO THE CITY COUNCIL
CITY OF CLARKSBURG, WEST VIRGINIA

First Annual Report Published

Among the, early events of the year just ended was the publication by the city council of the first annual report of Clarksburg under the Council-Manager plan of government.

The story of the past fiscal year, set forth in the pages that follow, will fall into the hands of many who did not receive the first report, for the year ending June 30, 1922. Its publication in pamphlet form has caused much favorable comment. For the first time in Clarksburg's history of 137 years, the people were taken into full confidence of their local government by the presentation of a year's work with the record, not only of what money was collected and spent, but of how the taxes were invested in service.

A brief summary of events and activities as noted in the first annual report under the present charter may serve as a preamble to its successor. During the year beginning July 1, 1921:

City debt was reduced $251,621;
Operating costs cut $22,484;
Modern detailed budget adopted;
City purchasing centralized;
Departmental reports required;
Complete penal code enacted;
Model sanitary code passed.

Police department reorganized;
Police court fines doubled;
Fire inspection emphasized;
Fire prevention taught in schools;
Many condemned buildings destroyed;
Fire loss reduced to 46 cents; (U. S. average, $4.41).

Full-time health department;
All contagious diseases reduced;
Health laboratory established;
Dairies inspected, milk tested;

Bacterial average reduced,
Cut from 7,500,000 to 90,000;
No baby deaths from bad milk;
Baby death rate 67 per 1,000;
Rigid sanitary inspection;
Over 300 dry closets abolished;
Bureau of vital statistics opened;
Waste collection system started;
Modern incinerator constructed;
Public charity systematized.

Improvement program made;
Completed $177,000 of work;
Four miles of sidewalk built;
Six bridges refloored for $9,000;
Four U. S. army trucks secured;
Roads graded and cindered;
Street lighting system extended;
Playground system started;
Library activities doubled;
Community team work developed.

Clarksburg City Council published the Second Annual Report of the City Manager to the City Council in 1923, complete with information about the First Annual Report. (Courtesy of the City of Clarksburg.)

City Officers and Employees 1922-1923

ADMINISTRATION AND FINANCE

City manager.........Harrison G. Otis
City attorney...........Fred L. Shinn
City clerk........Dolliver H. Hamrick
City treasurer.......Henry E. Reeder
Assistant treasurer....Robert F. Kuhl
Asst. collector....Brantley Rittenhouse
Stenographer........Alice Richardson
Janitor..................Paul Lunter

PUBLIC SERVICE DEPARTMENT

City engineer..........Thos. S. Lang
Construction eng'r..Mortimer W. Smith
Maintenance eng'r....Leon W. Collins
Construction foreman..Benj. W. Brown
Garbage superintendent....Bland Abell
Maintenance foremen........A. Gainer
  E. P. Gainer, Wm. Murphy,
  Chas. Huffman, W. H. Carson,
  and Burton Smith.

Truck drivers........Charles Heckert,
  W. A. Carson, L. E. Collins,
  D. R. Bramer, Harry Buchannon,
  T. L. McVaney.

Laborers, George Ashton, S. L. Bright,
  Coy Gainer, Bern Herbert, Thomas
  Huffman, E. M. Kelley, Frank Mc-
  Atee, James McAtee, Russell McClain,
  Eli Murphy, M. Phares, W. W. Pugh,
  John Smith, Leonard Smith.

POLICE DEPARTMENT

Police court judge......O. L. McDonald
Police chief...........Laco M. Wolfe
Lieutenant (reserve)..Michael F. Joyce
Desk sergeants........John T. Carter
      S. W. Stalnaker, Wm. J. Delson
Detective...........John L. Siers
Motorcycle police...Seymour Reynolds
  C. F. Montgomery, Thos. Cunningham
Patrolmen.......John Noon, H. L. Fox
  J. E. Shillinburg, E. F. Amsler, Jr.,
  Tom Feeney, D. Philbin, B. T. Keener,
  Frank Crutchfield, Thos. E. Lambert,
  J. E. Louchery, Ed. O. Henderson,
  H. M. Cookman, I. N. Cunningham,
Drivers....W. G. Olds, W. A. Sullivan
Dog catchers...Bob Brent, D. Howell

FIRE DEPARTMENT

Fire chief.............S. Ross Hoffman
Asst. Chiefs....R. H. Lee, D. L. Davis
Captains...M. M. Philbin, J. J. Martin,
  J. R. Riley, V. L. Groves, P. H. Taylor,
  C. W. Lantz, E. C. Teter, H. W. Pitts,
  H. H. Hamrick, W. T. Gainer,
  R. W. Bell, W. F. Carter, C. F. Hines,
  L. R. Shreve. J. H. Riggs

HEALTH DEPARTMENT

City physician....R. Linn Osborn, M.D.
Clerk.............Agnes F. Wilkinson
Food inspector..H. C. Williams, D.V.M.
Sanitary inspectors....John A. Tierney
    and John Caussain
City nurse..............Ethel McCarty
Bacteriologist.....Sol. L. Cherry, M. D.
Clinic director...Jas. T. Brennan, M. D.

WASTE COLLECTION and DISPOSAL
Crematory keepers.....James Schock,
  Adolph Schock, J. E. Layton.
Collection foremen.......Basil Bright,
  James Casto, Fred Hall.
Collectors................J. L. Bright.
  Charles Collins, M. Ogden, Ed. Rogers,
  Jos. Taylor, J. E. Stewart.

PUBLIC RECREATION

Director..............Fay H. Marvin
Asst. director.........Verne Matthew
Band leaders........Virgil W. Bork,
    and C. B. Writesel
Playgr'd leaders...Bernadette Brennan,
  Emma C. Smith, Clara W. Conrad,
  Wilma Smith, Marguerita Gardner,
  Helen Shuttleworth, Mary W. Collins,
  Alice Whelan, Nora K. Bell.

PUBLIC LIBRARY

City librarian.......Sally Scollay Page
Asst. librarians..Virginia S. Patterson,
    and May Potter.

This is a list of city officers and employees of the City of Clarksburg for the fiscal year 1922–1923, as it appeared in the city manager's Second Annual Report to City Council. (Courtesy of the City of Clarksburg.)

Sec. 26. Sale of weapons.[2]

On every license to sell or offer for sale pistols, revolvers, dirks, slung shots, billies, bowie knives, metallic or other false knuckles, or other weapons of like kind, the annual license fee shall be one hundred dollars. (1927, § 180; Ord. 6-16-37.)

Sec. 27. Shooting galleries.[3]

On every license to keep for public use or resort a shooting gallery the annual license fee shall be fifty dollars. (1927, § 190; Ord. 6-16-37.)

Sec. 28. Skating rinks.[4]

On every license to keep for public use or resort any skating rink the annual license fee shall be one hundred dollars. (1927, § 189; Ord. 6-16-37.)

Sec. 29. Slot machines.[5]

On every license to maintain any penny slot machine or other penny automatic device, which for the same profit or reward in each case, and without violation of law, furnishes facilities for weighing supplies or merchandise, or renders any service, the annual license fee shall be two dollars.

On every license to maintain any five-cent slot machine or other five-cent automatic device, which for the same profit or reward in each case, and without violation of law, furnishes music, the annual license fee shall be fifteen dollars.

On every license to maintain any five-cent slot machine or other five-cent automatic device, which for the same profit or reward in each case, and without violation of law, furnishes any amusement, except music, or affords the exercise of skill or the play of any game, the annual license fee shall be fifty dollars.

2. For state license tax upon the sale of weapons, see § 889 of Michie's West Virginia Code of 1943.

3. For state license tax upon shooting galleries, see § 883 of Michie's West Virginia Code of 1943.

4. For state license tax upon skating rinks, see § 881 of Michie's West Virginia Code of 1943.

5. For state license tax upon slot machines and automatic devices, see § 878 of Michie's West Virginia Code of 1943.

This is but one page excerpted from the Licenses and Taxation section of the City Code Book of the City of Clarksburg, published in 1944 when Roy F. Ash was city manager. (Courtesy of the City of Clarksburg.)

20

pavement or other public place, any printed, written, painted or other advertisement, bill, notice, sign or poster. (1927, 292.)

Sec. 2. Assault and battery.[6]

It shall be unlawful for any person to commit an assault or an assault and battery, or aid or encourage anyone in so doing. (1927, § 227.)

Sec. 3. Bicycles.

It shall be unlawful for any person to ride a bicycle upon any sidewalk in the city, or to ride a bicycle, with the feet of the rider removed from the pedals, or with both hands removed from the handlebars. (1927, § 279.)

Sec. 4. Children—Curfew.

It shall be unlawful for any child under the age of sixteen years to be upon the streets or in other public places of the city after the hour of ten o'clock P. M., unless accompanied by the parents, guardian or some adult person lawfully in charge of such child.

It shall be unlawful for any parent, guardian or other person having the custody of a child under the age of sixteen years, to allow such child to be upon the streets or in other public places in the city after ten o'clock P. M., unless accompanied by the parents, guardian or some adult person lawfully in charge of such child.

This section shall not be so construed as to prohibit children under sixteen years of age from attending places of religious worship or meetings held by or under the auspices of the public schools or boy scouts and girl scouts, or other like organizations unaccompanied by the parent, guardian or other adult person.

Any person violating any of the provisions of this section shall, upon conviction in the police court of the city, be fined not to exceed five dollars for the first offense, and for each succeeding offense thereafter shall be fined not less than five dollars, nor more than ten dollars, and in addition thereto may, in the discretion of the court, be imprisoned not to exceed ten days. (1927, §§ 245-248.)

---

6. For provisions of state law as to malicious and unlawful assaults, see §§ 5924 et seq. of Michie's West Virginia Code of 1943.

Here is another page of the Clarksburg City Code, taken from none other than the City Code Book of the City of Clarksburg, published in 1944. (Courtesy of the City of Clarksburg.)

REPORT ON
TOWN OF NORTH VIEW
North View, West Virginia

C O M M E N T S

EXHIBIT A - GENERAL FUND

TAXES $12,672.36

¶   Represents all the uncollected and assessed taxes
as shown by the last report dated January 31st, 1915, and the Tax
Receipt Books for years 1915-1916, the Capitation Tax being included.
The 1916 Assessors book was missing. The 1916 Tax Receipt Book does
not show the Capitation Taxes the same being carried in a separate
book.

   INTEREST ON TAXES $ 57.17

¶   Reflects the amount of interest collected on taxes
as taken from the stubs of the tax receipt books.

   FINES $ 545.02

¶   These amounts were compiled from the Mayor's Docket
for the years 1915 and 1916. The uncollected from the printed
report as at January 31st, 1915.

   LICENSE $ 280.84

¶   This is for license of Pool Rooms, Moving Pictures,
Drug Store, Etc.

   BOARDWALKS $ 781.16

¶   Reflects the amounts to be collected for Boardwalks
prior to January 31st, 1915, and amount charged in 1916. The records
do not show that any walks were charged to citizens during 1915.

When North View, now a section of Clarksburg, was a town in the early 20th century, a report
on business transacted appeared, prepared by the auditing firm of Willison Audit & System
Company, then located in the Goff Building. (Courtesy of the City of Clarksburg.)

Taxes Comparatively Low

Many people think of their city government first in terms of taxes. Moreover, some confuse state, county and school taxes with those received by the city. Lastly, most people consider taxes high. All things are high or low by comparison.

Comparison of cost with services received is the best method, but difficult to apply in all cases. This report gives some idea of what services the city administration is rendering. Comparison with the taxes paid in other cities of the state may be of interest. The accompanying table shows the total tax rates in thirty cities for last year.

Most People Pay More

Twenty-five of these thirty West Virginia cities have higher total tax rates than does Clarksburg. The average rate in all cities is $2.51, compared to our $1.96. That means that Clarksburg's citizens invest only 78 cents in schools, roads, public health, safety and the other forms of government where the average city dweller in this state invests $1.00.

WEST VIRGINIA TAX RATES, 1922

Richwood	$3.64
Sistersville	3.26
Williamson	3.03
Welch	3.055
Elkins	2.97
Buckhannon	2.96
Point Pleasant	2.935
Beckley	2.75
Princeton	2.75
Logan	2.705
Grafton	2.67
Bluefield	2.66
Follansbee	2.58
Wellsburg	2.58
Keyser	2.57
Moundsville	2.55
Hinton	2.545
Fairmont	2.41
Weston	2.35
Martinsburg	2.33
Morgantown	2.33
Mannington	2.25
S. Charleston	2.11
Wheeling	1.9935
Huntington	1.99
Clarksburg	1.96
Charleston	1.87
Parkersburg	1.85
Benwood	1.83
McMechen	1.83

Where Tax Money Goes

About one-third of the total tax comes to the city. In 1921-2 the increase was due to inherited debts and full time health department. In 1923-4 levies are added as follows: 10 cents for Adamston improvement project, ½ cent each for band music and firemen's pension.

Tax Distribution

City Tax	1920-1	1921-2	1922-3	1923-4
Admin. ...	19c	7c	6c	6 c
Police	8c	4c	3c	4 c
Fire	7c	10c	7c	7½c
Health	2c	3c	3c	3 c
Waste disp.	5c	4c	3c	1 c
Street care	11c	17c	13c	13 c
Street imp.	1c	1c	12c	21 c
St. lights..	6c	7c	5c	6 c
Recreation.	1c	0c	1c	1½c
Library....	1c	1c	1c	1 c
Debts, etc.,	23c	46c	12c	13 c
City rate	$.75	$1.00	$.66	$.77
State tax...	.20	.20	.15	.14
County tax	.60	.45	.27	.40
School tax.	1.34	1.33	.88	.86
Total rate.	$2.90	$2.98	$1.96	$2.17

Clarksburg ranked 26th in tax rates in 1922, according to this information taken from the Second Annual Report of the City Manager to City Council in 1923. (Courtesy of the City of Clarksburg.)

Until the early 1930s, the clock tower on the fourth Harrison County Courthouse was a predominant sight in downtown Clarksburg. (Courtesy of Dick Duez.)

The Nathan Goff National Guard Armory, which for years has hosted basketball games, exhibitions, and other events, was dedicated October 21, 1961.

The Army Reserve Center in Clarksburg stands on property between the Nathan Goff National Guard Armory and U.S. Route 19 south of the city.

Perhaps the largest manufacturing facility in the Clarksburg area is the UCar plant in Anmoore, shown in this aerial view. It was earlier known as the National Carbon Company and Union Carbide.

These employees of the Baltimore & Ohio Railroad pose for a photo during a work break. The B&O Depot was located on Baltimore Avenue in the Glen Elk section of Clarksburg, north of downtown. Today, Chessie Systems, or CSX, operates freight service only. (Courtesy of Dick Duez.)

This is the Hazel Atlas Glass Company plant in Clarksburg, which was located between the Adamston and North View sections of the city. It would later be named Continental Can Company, Brockway Glass Company, and Anchor Hocking Glass Company. The plant closed down in November 1987, leaving shy of 1,000 workers jobless. The remaining facilities were destroyed by perhaps the worst fire in Clarksburg's history in October 2000, which took months to completely extinguish. (Courtesy of Dick Duez.)

The West Fork Glass Company, which began business in 1905, is shown in this c. 1915 photo. It was located in the Industrial (Broadway) section of Clarksburg and was shut down in 1920. (Courtesy of Dick Duez.)

This pair of glassworkers appears inside the West Fork Glass Company plant in Clarksburg's Industrial section. (Courtesy of Dick Duez.)

The inside of Bert Stamm's grocery store shows many wares lining the walls. The store was located on Second Street in North View before the town incorporated into Clarksburg. (Courtesy of Dick Duez.)

Standard Advertising Corporation had its offices on West Pike Street near Angle Inn where Pike and West Main meet. The company handled outdoor advertising, more commonly known as billboards, in the Clarksburg area. This photo was taken in the 1930s, judging by the vehicle in the garage and the brick street. (Courtesy of Ronnie Smith.)

For many years, the Palace Furniture Company served the people of Clarksburg and central West Virginia at its 168 West Main Street location. The Palace opened in 1898 and remained open until the 1980s. The building stands today and houses a number of offices, including that of the Harrison County Chamber of Commerce. This photo was taken in 1935. (Courtesy of Ronnie Smith.)

The inside of the E.R. Davis & Company Hardware Store stood at 310–312 West Main Street in the middle of downtown Clarksburg. It operated from 1900 until 1929. (Courtesy of Harrison County Historical Society.)

Another downtown hardware store, photographed in 1950, was Roberts Hardware, which was located at 213 West Pike Street. The store opened in 1907 and closed some time in the 1970s. (Courtesy of Ronnie Smith.)

Here is the interior of what is believed to be Lowndes Bank in the very early 20th century in downtown Clarksburg. It stood, along with the R.T. Lowndes Department Store, at the corner of West Main and Third Streets for years. Eventually, the Lowndes Bank moved to more modern facilities on West Pike Street at the corner of Third Street, later became Community Bank & Trust, and today is the Clarksburg branch of Huntington Banks. (Courtesy of Harrison County Historical Society.)

Several gentlemen relax in the lobby of the Trader's Hotel, which was located at the southeast corner of West Main and South Third Streets in downtown Clarksburg. It opened in September 1895. A major blaze destroyed the hotel and other businesses housed in the structure on January 20, 1911. (Courtesy of Harrison County Historical Society.)

The Bee Hive department store, owned and operated by A.J. Fletcher, stood at 209–215 West Main Street in downtown Clarksburg from 1892 until 1919. From left to right in this c. 1900 photo are Margaret Leachman, Myrtle Leachman, Sandie Boyles, Elma Harris, Daisy White, and Mood Shepler. (Courtesy of Harrison County Historical Society.)

Friedlander's was a popular women's clothing retailer that was located on West Main Street at the corner of Fourth Street in downtown Clarksburg. The building was constructed after a blaze in February 1955 destroyed several businesses at the site. Today, it houses a church.

The Rolland brothers—Albert, Eugene, Ernest, Charles, and Aristide—are among the gentlemen photographed inside the plant of the Rolland Glass Company in Clarksburg. They acquired Peerless Window Glass Company in 1915 and formed the Rolland Glass Company. The company joined with the nearby Adamston Flat Glass Company and two out-of-state glass companies to form Fourco Glass Company. (Courtesy of Dick Duez.)

These were workers at the Adamston Flat Glass Company, shown in the "backyard" of the factory in the Adamston section of Clarksburg. The plant began operations in June 1926. (Courtesy of Dick Duez.)

Empire Building, Clarksburg, W. Va.

The Empire National Bank, at the corner of West Main and Fourth Streets in Clarksburg, opened in October 1903 in the Oak Hall Building, directly across the street. The bank moved into its new facilities in 1907, with Virgil Highland as the first president. The seven-story building is today occupied by Branch Banking & Trust Company (BB&T), with several other branch locations in the area. (Courtesy of Cris Green, Harrison County Historical Society president.)

The name of this restaurant on West Main Street at the corner of South Fifth Street could not be ascertained, but it is known to have housed a bonding and insurance company on the second floor. (Courtesy of Ronnie Smith.)

The Wonder Bar restaurant has for years stood at the top of a hill east of Clarksburg, with a magnificent view of the city. It was operated by the Folio family. (Courtesy of Harrison County Historical Society.)

The *Clarksburg Telegram* had its offices in this building on Fourth Street beside The Empire National Bank building. The photo appears to have been taken sometime in the very early 1920s or before. The Telegram Company bought out the Exponent Company in August 1927 and moved its offices to the Clarksburg Publishing Company building on Hewes Avenue. This photo graces the cover of this book. (Courtesy of the Harrison County Historical Society.)

The Waldo Hotel was once perhaps Clarksburg's most elegant hotel, standing at North Fourth and West Pike Streets downtown. Financed by Nathan Goff Jr., it was quite popular with out-of-town guests for many years.

The Hotel Gore opened for business in August 1913 on West Pike Street in Clarksburg and was another of the city's popular hotels.

Before U.S. Route 50 East became a four-lane highway in the late 1970s, the Colonial Court Motel on the old three-lane highway was a highly visible place for visitors to stay. The building is an office complex today.

Back when the sidewalks in downtown Clarksburg were considerably busier than they are today, this was a common sight: shoppers heading for their favorite stores. Although the buildings still stand, none of the businesses visible in this 1952 photo remains at this location. (Courtesy of Ronnie Smith.)

Clete Randolph, left, and John A. Snider, shown in 1936, were owners and partners of the West End Feed Company, which was located on the north end of the Milford Street Bridge in Clarksburg. The building was heavily damaged by fire in the early 1960s. (Courtesy of Bonnie Stalnaker.)

Jerry's Auto Supply and Sanitary Hot Dog, shown in 1957, were among the businesses located on the north side of West Pike Street near its intersection with North Third Street in downtown Clarksburg. The Burnside Foundation Museum and the Clarksburg Federal Building are at this site today. (Courtesy of Helen Wiles of Hepzibah.)

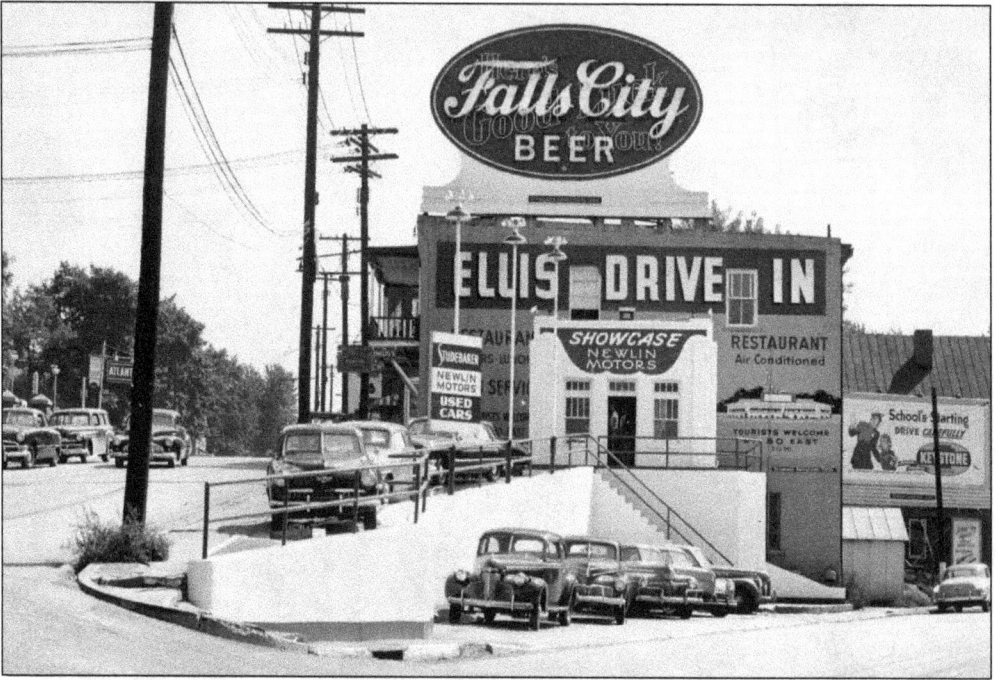

This 1952 photo shows Angle Inn, where West Pike and West Main streets converge in Clarksburg's West End. Newlin Motors, one of a number of automobile dealerships in the area, was a Studebaker dealer and also sold used cars, now known as "pre-owned automobiles." The neon Falls City sign was highly visible in the nighttime. (Courtesy of Ronnie Smith.)

One of the city's foremost men's clothiers was Melet's, previously known as the Will H. Melet Company. As the billboard says, the store sold Kuppenheimer clothes and Florsheim shoes. (Courtesy of Ronnie Smith.)

The Tin Plate Mill, shown here, was located in Despard, just east of Clarksburg. First named the Jackson Sheet and Tin Plate Company, J.R. Phillips came to the area to operate the plant, renaming it the Phillips Sheet and Tin Plate Company. It was said to be the largest manufacturing enterprise in central West Virginia in its heyday.

Looking north, this aerial photo shows Interstate 79 at its interchange with U.S. Route 50. The large, light-shaded property is where the Eastpointe I shopping center is located today. The site of Eastpointe II, much smaller in area, can be seen on the north side of Route 50.

The Lowndes Building, shown in this 1961 photograph, housed the Lowndes Bank and Parsons-Souders Department Store. When the bank moved to more modern facilities in 1965, the department store remained, named Stone & Thomas Department Store. The building was demolished in the 1990s to make way for a new Clarksburg municipal building.

Here's a 1961 diagonal view of the lower stories of the Stonewall Jackson Hotel and the Union National Bank, with the Wilbur Marr jewelry store located between them. The building is all part of Bank One today. Modoc Alley is in the foreground at right.

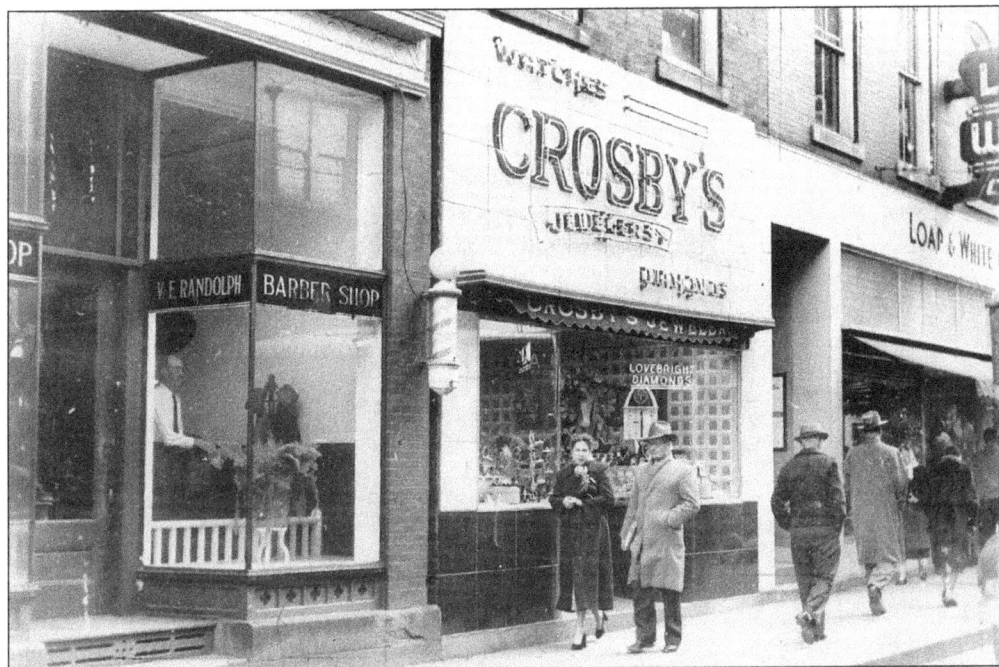

The storefronts of W.E. Randolph's Barber Shop, Crosby's Jewelers, and Loar & White men's clothiers appear in this photo taken in 1952 on South Third Street downtown. (Courtesy of Ronnie Smith.)

Looking westward up West Main Street, this photo shows both Watts-Sartor-Lear and Parsons-Souders department stores on the right-hand side of the street. The structure at left in the background is the Goff Building.

This is the interior of one of several jewelry stores that were located in downtown Clarksburg in the late 19th and early 20th centuries. (Courtesy of Dick Duez.)

Ray's Snack Bar, located directly across West Pike Street from Victory High School in Adamston, was a favorite meeting place for students and others. (Courtesy of Paul O. Hill.)

Three

THE CITY WE KNEW

Most of the images in Clarksburg that appear in this chapter represent an era with which people of the baby boomer years and older can readily identify. They are from a period that many may consider as less complicated, a time when folks could leave their front doors unlocked without fear of someone breaking in to burglarize the house. Herein are some aerial views of the downtown Clarksburg area from the north, south, east, and west that show, for example, when Saint Mary's Hospital was still standing at South Chestnut Street and Washington Avenue, when the Clarksburg parking garage was merely an architect's idea, or when Route 50 East was a three-lane—not a four-lane—highway with businesses on both sides. For all practical purposes, these pages show a city we can truly say that we knew.

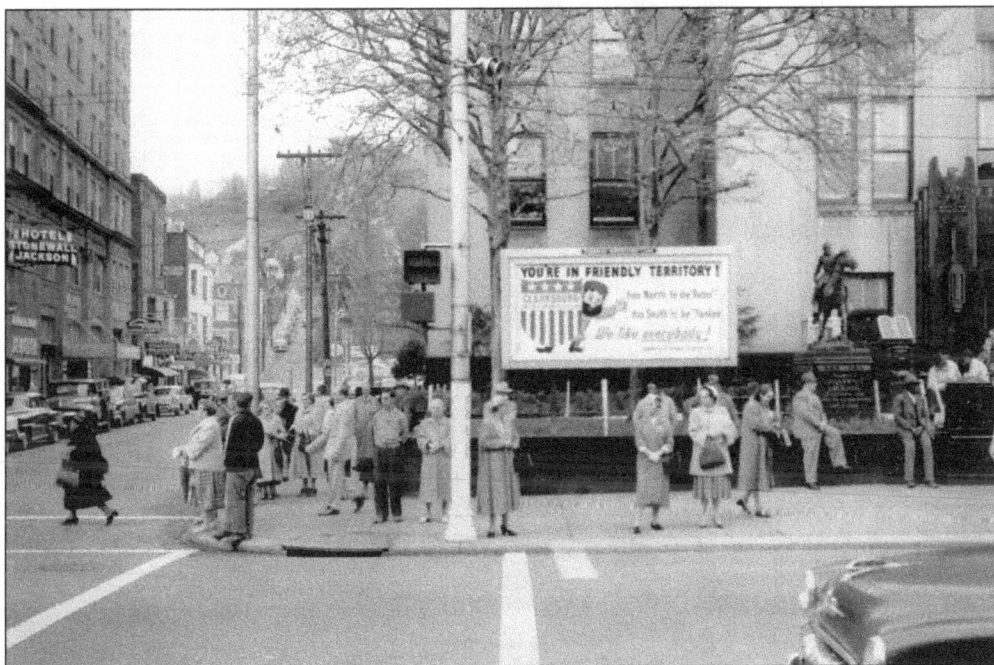

Business people and shoppers scurry along or just wait for a bus or cross the street at the corner of West Main and South Third Streets in downtown Clarksburg, just in front of the Harrison County Courthouse. The Stonewall Jackson Hotel can be seen at far left. (Courtesy of Harrison County Historical Society.)

The makings of a mammoth traffic jam appear in this photo taken in the early 1950s in Clarksburg's West End. At left are Roger Roberts's Esso service station, Kroger's supermarket, a Dairy Queen, and some apartment buildings. In the background is Pierpont Elementary School. (Courtesy of Harrison County Historical Society.)

A new YWCA center is shown under construction in 1961 on Washington Avenue, across from the Harrison County Jail. The parking lot to the right was owned by the Union National Bank and used for its customers.

The Empire National Bank building
and the Saint Charles Hotel
are plainly visible in this photo
taken from the Goff Building on
West Main Street in Clarksburg.
(Courtesy of Dick Duez.)

The ladies carried umbrellas and the men wore hats to protect themselves from the sun as they
stood in groups on West Pike Street in front of what is now Waldomore and alongside the Waldo
Hotel in this turn-of-the-century photo. (Courtesy of Harrison County Historical Society.)

U.S. Route 50 East is shown in two separate sections. The photo above shows the highway between Clarksburg and Bridgeport, and below is Route 50 just a few short years after the Clarksburg Expressway was built. Both pictures were taken in 1961. Visible at right in the photo below are the Immaculate Conception Catholic Church and Notre Dame High School. For several years after the expressway was built, its eastern terminus was on East Pike Street near its intersection with Park Street.

Downtown Clarksburg was a bustling place when photographed in 1971. In the foreground at left are the C&P Telephone Company Building, the Curtain Shop, and Ora Batchellor clothiers on the ground floor of the Colonial Apartments; a partially hidden Pursglove Coal Company; and, beyond that, the Empire National Bank. In the foreground at right flies Old Glory in front of what was then city hall. Past the trees is the Firestone Tires store. The tall structure at right is the Goff Building.

The back of Towers Elementary School, as well as numerous residences, the Hotel Gore, the Prunty Building, the Union National Bank building, and the Goff Building were photographed

Evergreens flank this part of the Sunny Croft Country Club, located along U.S. Route 19 south of Clarksburg. Another golf club, the Clarksburg Country Club, is located just a short distance away.

sometime in the first half of the 20th century. Lowndes Hill is in background. (Courtesy of Jean Murphy of Bridgeport and Frances Givens of Carmichael, California.)

Folks walk alongside a Baltimore & Ohio Railroad passenger train near Baltimore Avenue in Glen Elk. Passenger train service was discontinued in Clarksburg several years ago.

Can there be any wonder why this area, virtually surrounded by the West Fork River, was known for years as River Bend Park? The building near the top of the photo is today the Louis A. Johnson Veterans Administration Medical Center, which was known when photographed as simply the Veterans Hospital. A new bridge has been planned upstream to replace the deteriorating span shown at bottom right. The roadway through the park, now part of West Virginia Route 98, is known to this day as the V.A. Straight.

A crane rises near the base of the structure on Hewes Avenue, beside Towers Elementary School, which would later become the Clarksburg parking garage. The eastbound Third Street on- and off-ramps of the Clarksburg Expressway, as well as the westbound Second Street on- and off-ramps, pass beneath the garage. The building at left is now occupied by Clarksburg Printing Company. (Courtesy of Fred Layman.)

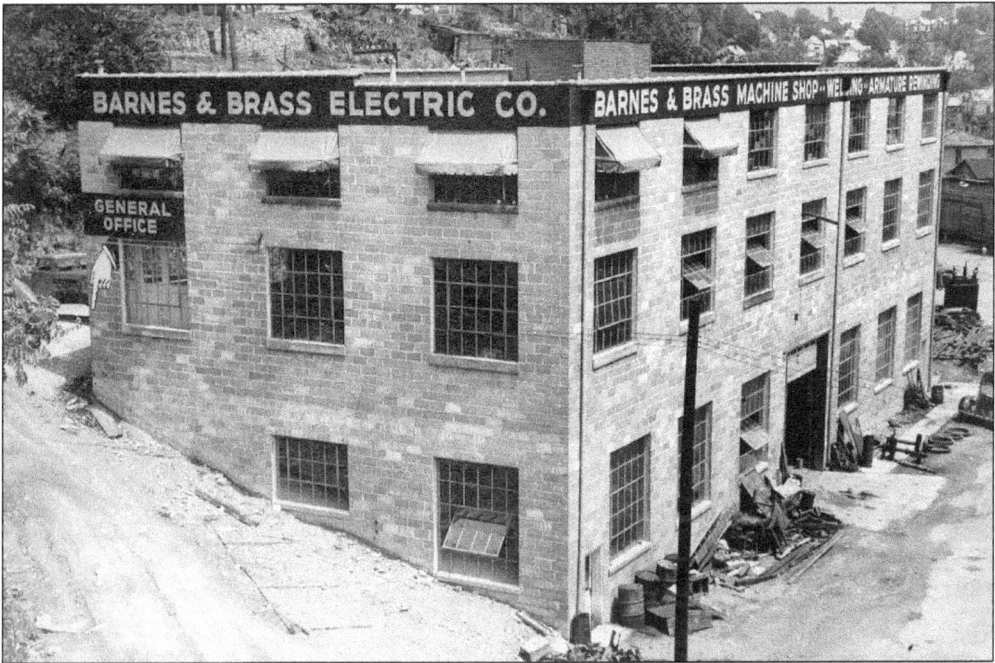

Barnes & Brass Electric Company, near the intersection of North Fourth and Ford Streets in Glen Elk, is shown in this photograph that was taken probably 50 or more years ago. The building and the business are still in existence today. The Clarksburg Police Department had its temporary headquarters in the building around 30 years ago. (Courtesy of Harrison County Historical Society.)

This familiar sight at the south end of the Fourth Street Bridge is Clarksburg's bus terminal. Local City Lines buses, as well as Greyhound and various touring buses, used the terminal. A new CENTRA bus facility was recently constructed beside the old bus station.

The UpTowner Inn was located in the 100 block of West Main Street in the late 1960s and early 1970s, later becoming the Sheraton Inn. It would continue as the Sheraton for about 10 years and was the prime meeting and banquet headquarters in Clarksburg for some time. Today, it is the John W. Davis State Office Building. (Courtesy of Harrison County Historical Society.)

The Clarksburg Branch of the United States Postal Service and United States District Courthouse is a long name indeed for a building, but that's it as it appeared in 1961. However, an expansion was added several years later, with a parking lot for customers near West Pike Street. The expansion was built on the site where Queen's Pure Oil service station was located for years. The building across the street was the Lynch-Stacy Funeral Home.

Gabberts' Esso service station and parking lot can be seen in the foreground of this 1961 photo. Just behind the Esso sign is the building that housed various television cable companies that served Clarksburg over the years. The building with the twin white bays is the Leggett Building, followed by the Knights of Pythias Building, the Stonewall Jackson Hotel, and the Union National Bank.

Like a long, white ribbon, the Clarksburg Expressway (U.S. Route 50) passes from left to right across this bird's-eye view of the city, taken in the 1960s. The buildings of the Glen Elk section of Clarksburg can be seen at the right, with Montpelier Addition in the center foreground. Downtown Clarksburg is, of course, to the left of the bridges. Suburban areas such as Stealey and Point Comfort appear in the background. (Courtesy of Harrison County Historical Society.)

Residences in the Glenwood Hill Addition of Clarksburg are at left, with North View in the right background, as a train snakes its way just above the Wilsonburg Road, not visible in the photo. (Courtesy of Dick Duez.)

Cars are shown in Edgar White's mid-city parking lot, photographed in the 1950s. The buildings shown housed the popular Manhattan Restaurant, the Evans Hotel, at least two poolrooms, and upstairs apartments. (Courtesy of Harrison County Historical Society.)

These folks are about to board the train as they are assisted by B&O Railroad personnel at the Clarksburg depot on Baltimore Avenue in the Glen Elk section.

Sears, Roebuck & Company and the Palace Furniture Company are among the buildings at left as traffic passes eastbound on West Main Street. At right is Westminster Hall of the First Presbyterian Church in Clarksburg.

Built in the very early 20th century was the Benevolent and Protective Order of Elks Lodge 482 in downtown Clarksburg, shown in 1961. The lodge was flanked at the left by the Monongahela Power store and at right by the Masonic Temple, which still stands. The Elks Lodge was destroyed by fire in late 2000.

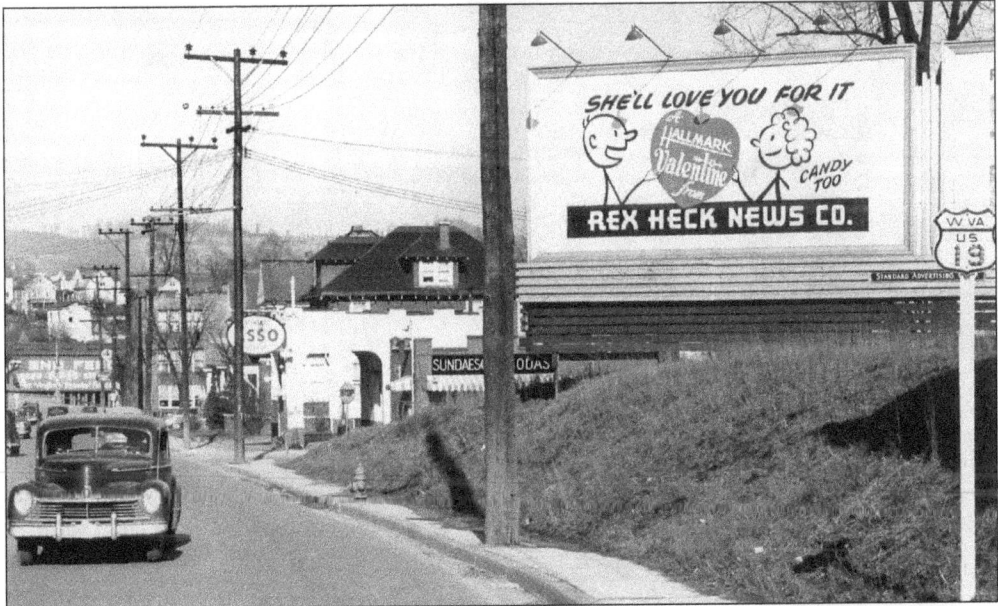

Milford Street (U.S. Route 19) in the Stealey section of Clarksburg has long been a heavily-traveled thoroughfare. Much of this scene has changed since this photo was taken, probably in the late 1940s. The small, grassy hill at right has long since been leveled and today is the site of a Dairy Queen Brazier restaurant. The Stealey Barber Shop has replaced the Esso station, and the brick apartments in the background were demolished in 2004. Also visible is a portion of the West End Feed Store. (Courtesy of Ronnie Smith.)

The exact location of this three-story brick building in Clarksburg, with a sheet metal business on the ground floor, could not be readily determined. It is known, however, that it was neither the Leggett Building nor the Rookery Apartments (both on opposite page), which were separated only by a brick house on South Third Street downtown. (Courtesy of Dick Duez.)

The building shown above was the original Leggett Building on South Third Street, which was built by Clarence Wheeler Leggett at the turn of the 20th century. It was said to be the first three-story building to be constructed in the city on the south side of Elk Creek. For $1 and other considerations, the building was given to the Knights of Pythias, and the K of P, in turn, sublet the ground floor to Stonewall Billiards, owned by Ray and Al Heck, and to the Blue Bird Store, which was then owned by Carl Futuro and subsequently sold to Frank X. Lopez. The structure at left, the Rookery Apartments, subsequently became the Leggett Building. (Courtesy of Robert Neeley.)

The brick building in the center of this photo, taken by Louis Hill, is Saint Mary's Hospital, which, along with the Union Protestant Hospital four blocks away, served the people of Clarksburg, Harrison County, and central West Virginia. The building was demolished in the late 1970s after patients were transferred to the United Hospital Center, along U.S. Route 19 South. The picture was taken near the intersection of South Chestnut Street and Lee Avenue. Note the "Quiet Hospital Zone" sign in the foreground. (Courtesy of Paul O. Hill.)

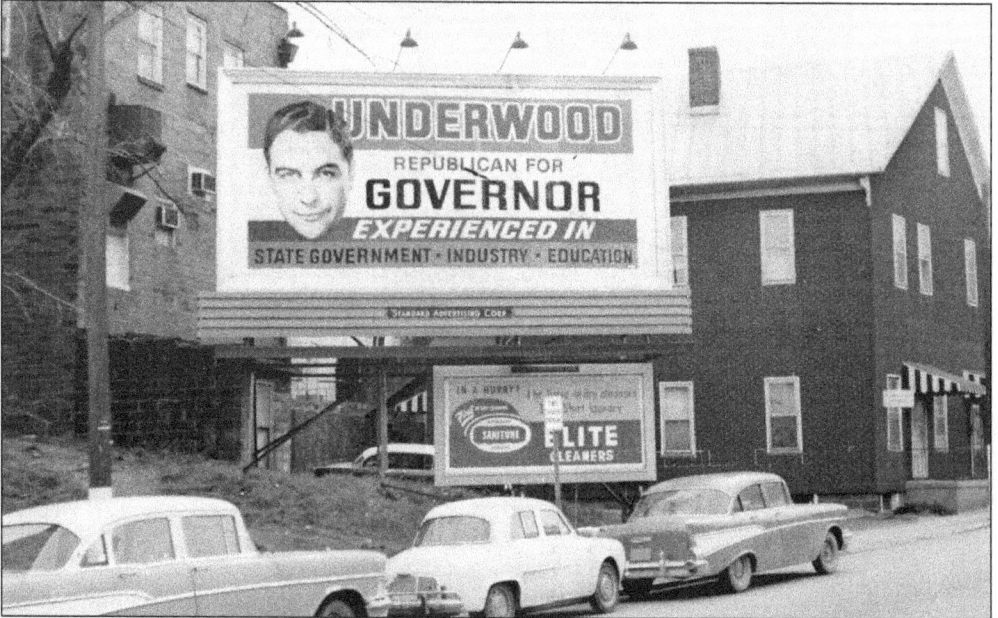

This was a campaign billboard supporting Cecil H. Underwood for governor in 1956. It was located along West Main Street, near the angle with West Pike Street. Underwood, of Sistersville, was elected and served as West Virginia's governor from 1957 to 1961, the state's youngest governor in its history. Forty years later, Underwood was elected to his second term as governor, from 1997 to 2001, also becoming the oldest person in state history to be elected governor. (Courtesy of Ronnie Smith.)

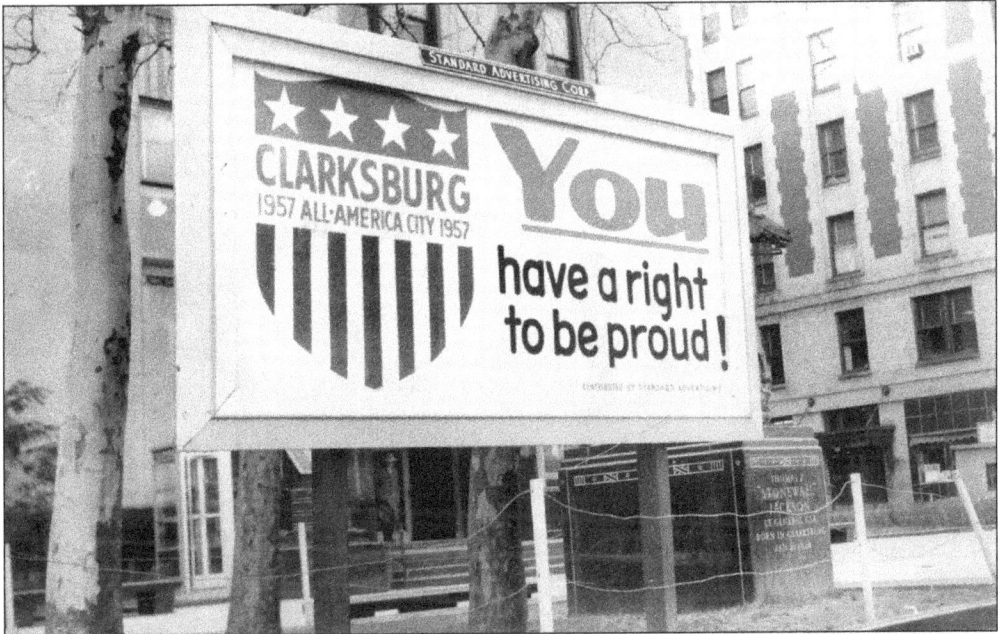

Clarksburg was named All-America City in 1957, and this signboard proclaimed that Clarksburg residents "have a right to be proud." E.W. James was mayor of the city at the time. The sign was located beside the statue of Stonewall Jackson on the Harrison County Courthouse Plaza. (Courtesy of the Harrison County Historical Society.)

A look at Clarksburg today from Lowndes Hill, for example, would be considerably different from this scene. At extreme left is the steepled Harrison County Courthouse, which was demolished in the early 1930s. The main street shown in this photo is Second Street, with the First Presbyterian Church's spire in the center. The other large building at the end of Second Street is believed to be Towers School.

63

This is yet another photo looking up West Main Street in downtown Clarksburg from its intersection with Second Street. Several other businesses can be seen from this vantage point.

The north side of West Pike Street in the 400 block includes Ideal (photographic) Studio, the People's Store, a building containing a barber shop, and the Ritz News and the Ritz Theater, indicated by the marquee. A City Lines bus is seen loading and unloading passengers, and in the background at left is the Waldo Hotel.

Looking to the east is this bird's-eye view of Clarksburg. The Sixth Street Bridge is in foreground at left, after which is the Fourth Street Bridge and the Second Street ramp and bridge. This was in about 1966, when the Clarksburg Expressway ended at East Pike Street. Saint Mary's Hospital is in the foreground toward the right. Just above it in the picture is Washington Irving High School, now W.I. Middle School. Looking clockwise near the top left of the photo are Montpelier Addition, East End, Goff Plaza, Industrial, and Broad Oaks.

Birds Eye View of Clarksburg, W. Va.

Yet another view of Clarksburg looking north is shown in this illustration, this time looking down South Third Street. (Courtesy of Harrison County Historical Society.)

The Easter Seals Society's Crippled Children's Center was located on Liberty Avenue in Clarksburg's Hartland section for quite a number of years.

Easily distinguishable in this aerial photo is Hite Field, which has rarely gone without a Friday football game during the scholastic grid season for more than 50 years. At top left is the former Monticello Elementary School on Frederick Street. South Chestnut Street is seen in the left portion of the photograph. Sutter Roofing and various other business interests can be seen in the right foreground. The West Fork River and the Hartland section can be seen in the center at the top of the photo.

This picture postcard illustration shows Pike Street in 1910, but exactly which block of Pike it is cannot be detected. On the left side of the street were a poolroom, the Pike News Company, and Model Liquor Store, and at right is the *Clarksburg News* office. (Courtesy of Harrison County Historical Society.)

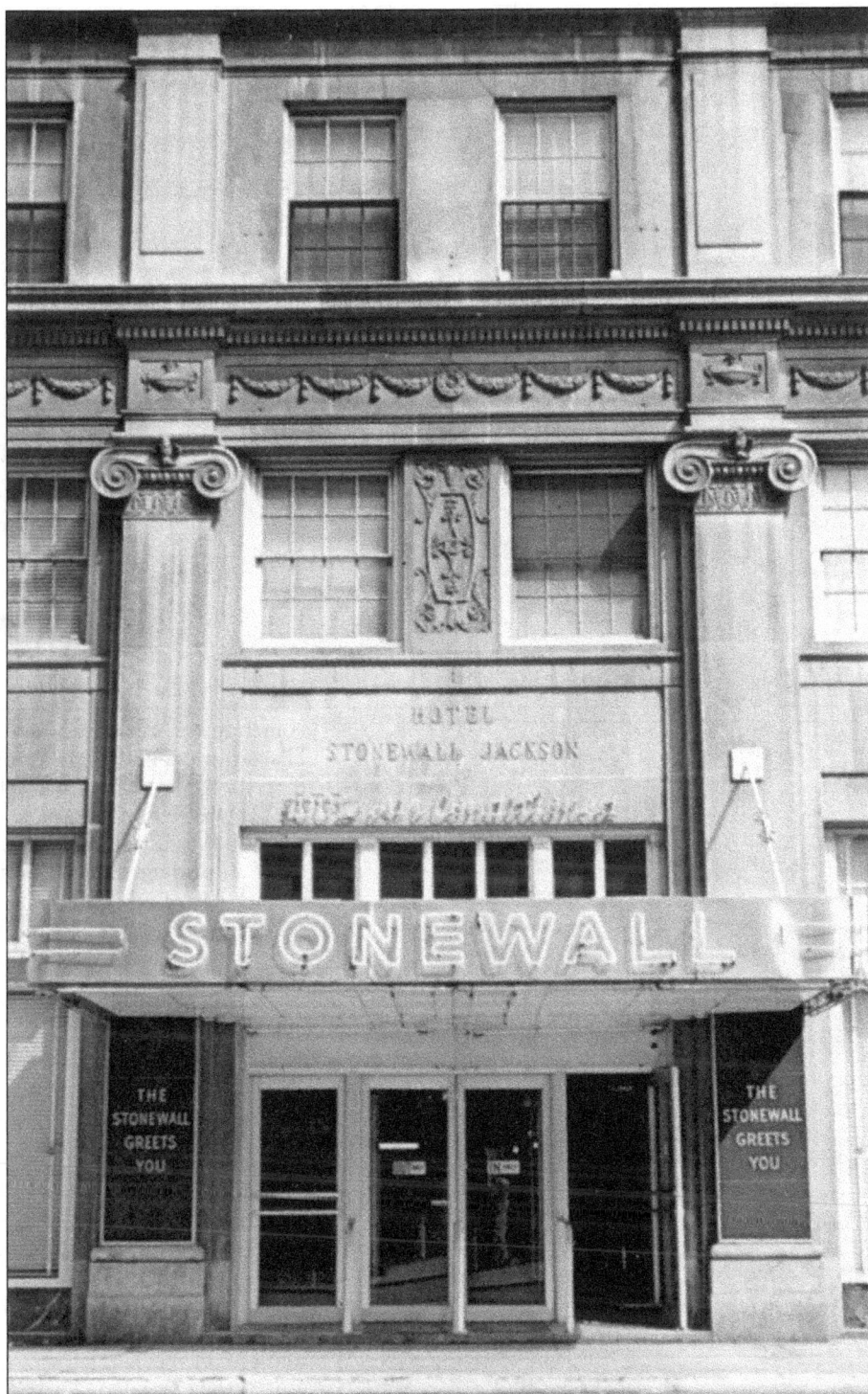

Here's an "in-your-face" glance at the entrance to the Stonewall Jackson Hotel on South Third Street downtown. Many a function took place in the hotel's ballroom, and the Mirror Room was also a center of attraction to visitors.

Fourth Street, between Main and Pike streets, appears here as it did in 1910. Barely visible at far left is the Empire National Bank, and at right midway down the block is a home furnishings store. (Courtesy of Dick Duez.)

The Goff Building, which stands beside the Harrison County Courthouse, was built in 1911 by Nathan Goff Jr. Through the years, it has housed the office suites of doctors and lawyers, as well as the Clarksburg Chamber of Commerce offices and Aaron's Shoe Store. The building remains a prominent sight today.

Four

HOME—WHERE THE HEART IS

Clarksburg is a place where a number of fine, old homes are located. Some of the houses that were well known in the city have long since been demolished, and photographs of all could not be procured for use in this work. Some of the houses were Victorian in style, while others had a style all their own. They were the homes of well-known Clarksburg citizens. Sometimes, several houses of a certain style of architecture could be found in the same neighborhood, while in other cases, a house might be the only one of its kind on the street. Unfortunately, only a limited number of photos of those houses were available.

This is a view of a nice neighborhood in Clarksburg. It shows some old homes on Mulberry Avenue in Clarksburg. (Courtesy of Harrison County Historical Society.)

71

The Harrison County Chapter of the American Red Cross was organized in April 1917 during a special meeting at the courthouse. This is the chapter headquarters, located at 165 South Oak Street in Clarksburg, which was formerly a residence. (Courtesy of Harrison County Historical Society.)

STANLEY AVENUE, GOFF PLAZA, CLARKSBURG, W. VA.

These are some homes on Stanley Avenue in Clarksburg's Goff Plaza section in the early 20th century. Many of the homes still stand today. (Courtesy of Harrison County Historical Society.)

Partially hidden by maple trees, this is the Stealey home at 601 Milford Street in Clarksburg. It is one of the oldest homes in the Stealey section of Clarksburg.

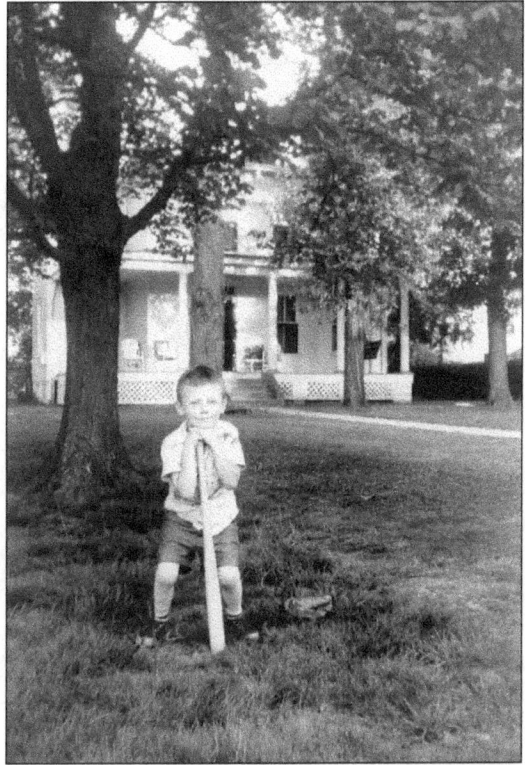

This is the First Church of Christ Scientist, 658 West Pike Street in Clarksburg, as it looked in the 1880s. Among those pictured are Mrs. Joseph F. Osborn and son, Robert Linn Osborn. Joseph F. Osborn bought the house in 1853 from Lloyd Lowndes. It remained Osborn property until 1937, when Dr. Robert Linn Osborn sold it to the church. The structure was probably built in the 1820s or 1830s. (Courtesy of Robert Maxwell.)

Next door to the Burton Despard house, which is now Davis-Weaver Funeral Home, is the residence known as the Dr. Joseph Carr house. It is located on East Main Street at the corner of Carr Avenue, which was named for the doctor. (Courtesy of Dick Duez.)

Little is known about the location of the residence shown above; it is said to have been owned by the Hood family, and the damage that can be seen at the back of the home apparently resulted from a fire. (Courtesy of Dick Duez.)

Here is the mantle in the parlor of the Hall residence in Clarksburg as it appeared in 1911. Information on the family and the location of the home was not available. (Courtesy of Dick Duez.)

This is the Ross F. Stout house, at 260 E. Main Street on what is known as "Quality Hill" in Clarksburg. At right was once the residence of Dr. James T. Brennan, a well-known and respected physician in the Clarksburg area. The Quinn home would subsequently become the McGlumphy Mortuary. (Courtesy of Dick Duez.)

At 512 Milford Street in Clarksburg stood the Nicholas Carpenter house. Members of the Stealey family would perform music for many years in a band that was directed by their father, John E. Stealey. From left to right are Mary Temple Stealey, Charles T. Stealey, Eunice Stealey, Elizabeth Stealey, Lelia Stealey, Irvin Ray Stealey (the author's grandfather), Joseph E. Stealey, Ethel Stealey, and John E. Stealey. (Courtesy of Harrison County Historical Society.)

The fine old Queen Anne structure above was known as the Perry C. Williams house. On East Main Street, it was one door west of the Quinn House and would later be the Petitto residence. (Courtesy of Dick Duez.)

Five

A CITY AND ITS PEOPLE

Make no mistake about it, the greatest resource of a city—Clarksburg certainly included—is its people. Their ideas and creativity make their city move forward. It is they who served. It is they who, while perhaps ordinary citizens, were our neighbors. In this day of high technology and computers, it is people who continually remind us that while some computers are made to solve many of the world's hardest problems, only the people have the capacity to discern the situations of the heart and soul. Just as it was in our earlier days, it is the people upon whom we can count as our friends.

These gentlemen, all wearing caps or hats as was the custom in the early 20th century, pose for the photographer just outside a phonograph/music store somewhere in Clarksburg. (Courtesy of Dick Duez.)

The Stealey Playground has for years been a popular place to congregate and recreate. These children, pictured in August 1944, were frequent visitors to the playground and were under the direction of Catherine Rose Custer.

Here's the author of this book, Bob Stealey, caught on camera at age 11 walking along Stealey Avenue near his home.

These folks are members of the Jackson family, meeting behind their home on Monticello Avenue in Clarksburg. The older lady in the back row, who was unidentified, was said to have lived to the age of 107. (Courtesy of Janice McPherson.)

The Meuse-Argonne Post 573 home of the Veterans of Foreign Wars in Clarksburg was the site of this dinner meeting that consisted of several law enforcement officers. None of those pictured could be identified. (Courtesy of Dick Duez.)

The Saint Paul's Methodist Episcopal Church at West Main and Chestnut Streets in Clarksburg is where these Sunday school children and adults gathered to have their photo taken. No identification of the members was available. The building now houses the Seventh Day Adventist Church of Clarksburg. (Courtesy of the Harrison County Historical Society.)

Andy Grisso is surrounded by his grandchildren, from left to right, Lester Rokisky, Eleanor Rokisky, Tony Yonovak, and Mary Yonovak, in the mid-1930s. Young Tony was crying because he wanted to drive the car. (Courtesy of Mary Yonovak.)

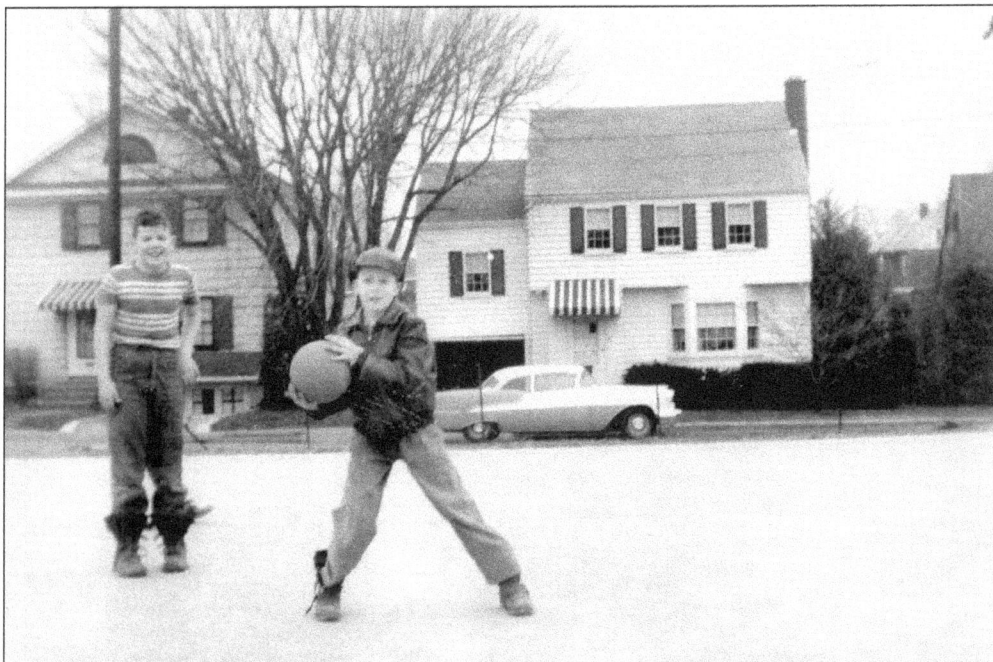

These youngsters appear to be practicing basketball on the court at the Stealey Playground on Milford Street. They are Dave Watson, at left, and John Hutton, with the ball. Houses on Hall Street appear in the background.

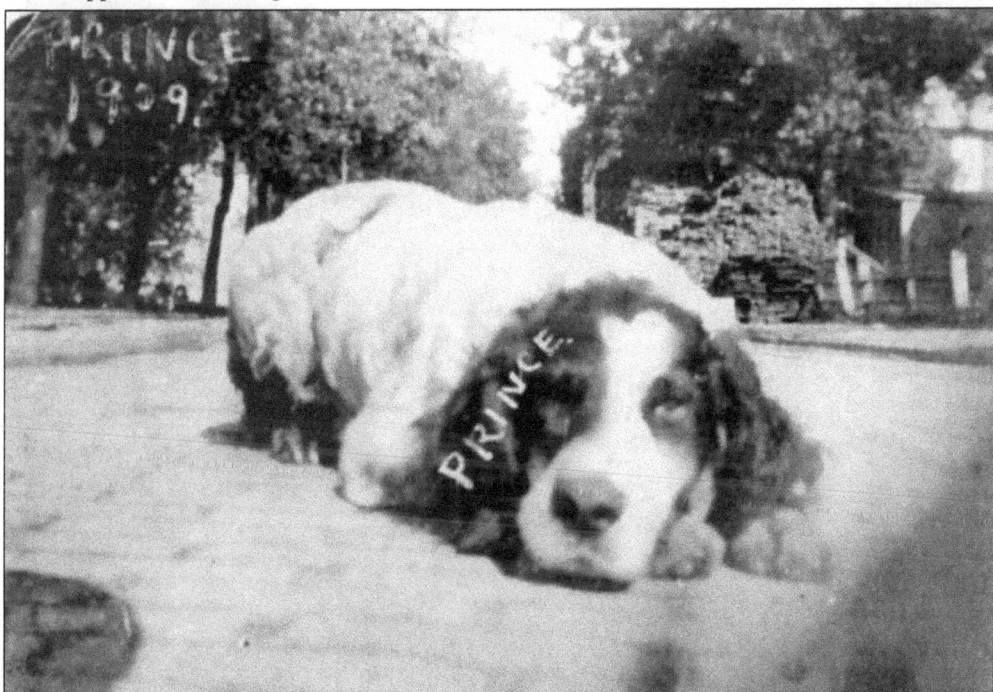

On which street Prince the English springer spaniel decided to take his nap couldn't be determined, but it appears that Prince doesn't really care. The photo was taken in 1909. (Courtesy of Dick Duez.)

Ruth Lawrence (Bellotte) and Barbara Insani pose for the photographer on the old swinging bridge between North View and Adamston, sometime between 1949 and 1951. The Adamston Flat Glass Company plant is seen in the background. (Courtesy of Ruth Lawrence Bellotte.)

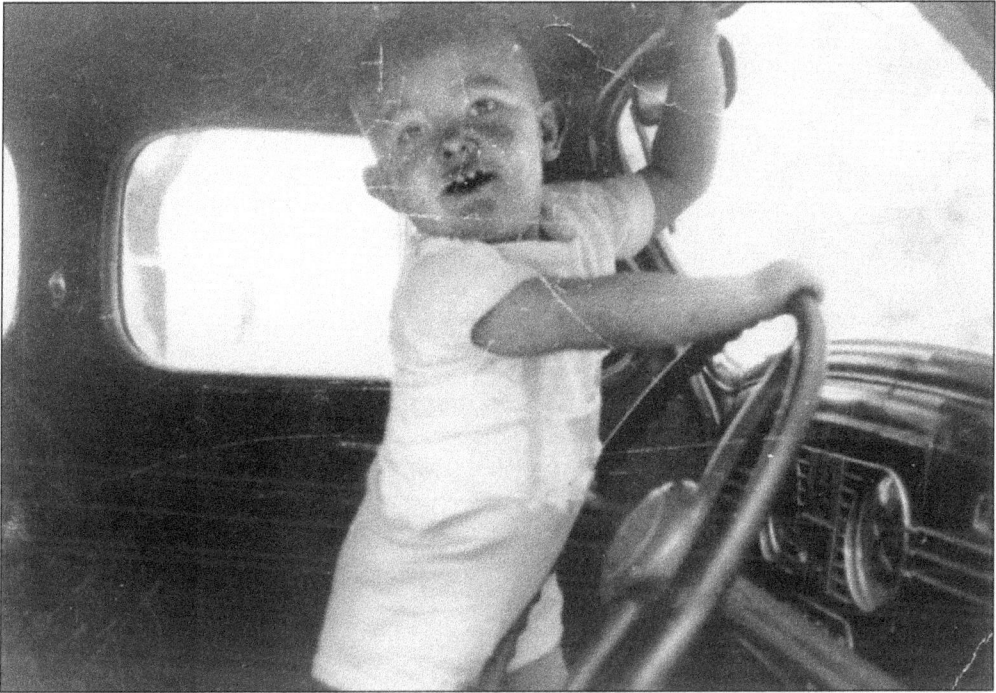

Three-year-old Fred R. "Dick" Hall must have decided to be just like his dad, Clarence Everett "Buss" Hall of Clarksburg, when he took the wheel of the family car back in the 1940s. (Courtesy of Janice Hall McPherson.)

Granville Davisson Hall, author of the novel *Daughter of the Elm*, is seated reading his newspaper sometime around Christmas in 1909. The book is quite well known, especially in central West Virginia. Its setting was the Big Elm community just north of Shinnston. Hall also wrote *Old Gold*. (Courtesy of the Harrison County Historical Society.)

Robert Maxwell is pole-vaulting a height of about eight feet in his grandfather's, Judge Haymond Maxwell, backyard at 608 East Main Street in Clarksburg's Goff Plaza section. Note that he is in his stocking feet and street clothes. The pole is a rug pole from the Palace Furniture Company. (Courtesy of Robert Maxwell.)

The four Ellis brothers appear here in the restaurant they owned and operated at the foot of Bridgeport Hill in front of their drive-in theater. From left to right, they are Joe, Sam, Louie, and

Here is a portrait of Mrs. Ora Earl
Coffman, who was a long-time
resident of the Clarksburg area.
Her appearance in the photo would
date the image to sometime in the
very early part of the 20th century.
(Courtesy of Janice Hall McPherson.)

John Ellis, and they were known as the "Brothers Four." In addition to that restaurant, they also
owned the Sunset-Ellis Restaurant on U.S. Route 19 between Clarksburg and Shinnston.

John W. Davis of Clarksburg, nominee for president of the United States in 1924, doffs his hat for the photographer, Mrs. Anna Virginia (Rector) Murphy, during his return visit to his home town on August 10, 1924. He is standing at the corner of South Third Street and Lee Avenue near his residence. Others in the photo could not be identified. (Courtesy of the Harrison County Historical Society.)

This is a photo of Clarence Everett "Bus" Hall, long a resident of Clarksburg's Broad Oaks section, in his United States Navy uniform. Hall served his country in World War II. (Courtesy of Janice Hall McPherson.)

This old-time automobile must have been the pride and joy of Ed Hart, shown outside his residence in 1911. (Courtesy of Dick Duez.)

Will Cody and John Kane look sporty on the banks of the Elk Creek one fair Sunday in July 1910. (Courtesy of Janice Hall McPherson.)

C.E. Wilson Company, a specialty photography studio located in Clarksburg, took this portrait of local resident Ora Earl Coffman at an early age sometime near the turn of the 20th century. (Courtesy of Janice Hall McPherson.)

88

Six

THERE WHEN WE NEEDED THEM

Firefighters, police officers, paramedics, and emergency medical technicians: they are the ones who have so unselfishly devoted their lives to helping others in the midst of dire circumstances. After all, where would we be without the first responders in times of emergency? In times past, such individuals may not have had available to them all the modern marvels of their professions, but they've always had the presence of mind and heart to make life a little easier for their fellow humans. The following images reflect the entities of yesterday that, in their own day, were the most modern means of assisting others when they sought help.

The Clarksburg Fire Department's aerial and pumper trucks look ready to answer an alarm at any time in front of the Central Station. The department has three other stations—East End, West End, and North View sub-stations. In later years, the arched doorways shown here were renovated, heightened a bit, and squared off.

Clarksburg Fire Department had an emergency car (ambulance), pictured here in the 1940s, up until the early 1960s. In fact, in the 1950s, CFD had at least two emergency cars available when needed. (Courtesy of Clarksburg Fire Department.)

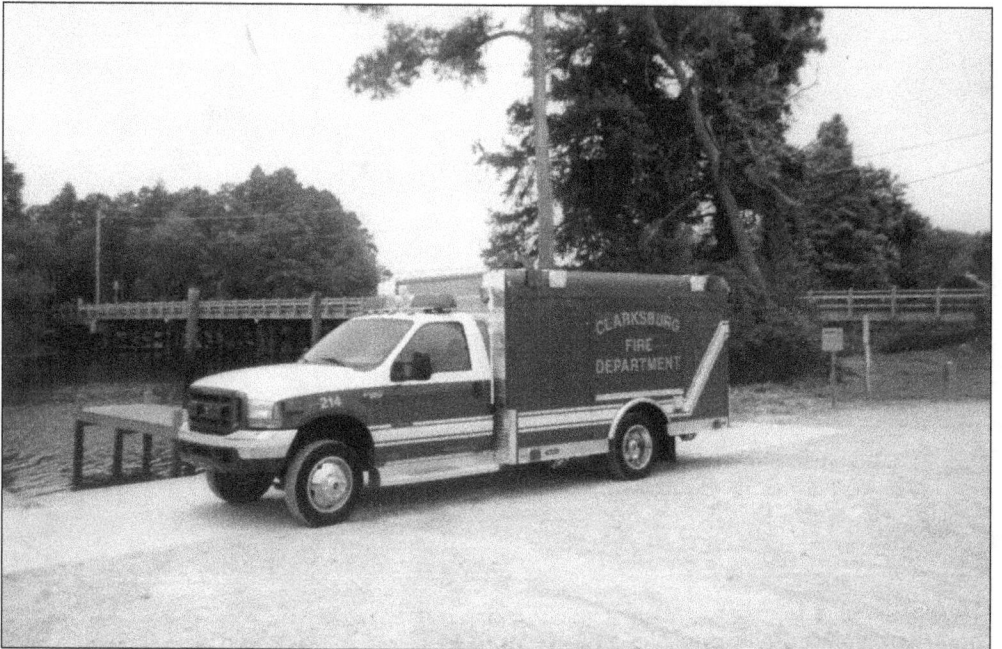

In the late 1990s or early in the 21st century, Clarksburg Fire Department had a rescue truck available for fires, traffic accidents, and medical emergencies. CFD has acquired an even newer rescue truck since this photo was taken. (Courtesy of Clarksburg Fire Department.)

These were the members of the Clarksburg Police Department in 1975. Some of those shown here are members even today. From left to right are (first row) narcotics agent Jim Hendrickson, detective Larry Robey, detective Sgt. Jack Chipps, detective Lt. Gene Conaway, detective Steve Toryak, and narcotics agent Ron Kirby; (second row) Lt. Raymond Muscatell, Lt. Charles Reich, Lt. Francis Muscatell, Lt. George D. Shields, and Lt. Frank J. Paletta; (third row) police chief Sam J. Paletta and police court judge Sam B. Kyle Jr.; (fourth row) Sgt. Joe M. Fuscaldo, Sgt. George Stackpole, Sgt. Daniel H. Amsler, Sgt. Herman Kesling Jr., and Sgt. Jerry Robey; (sixth row) patrolmen Joseph Luzader, Dale Cain, Dennis Mazza, Stanley Chipps, Clifford Floyd, and William Grant; (seventh row) patrolmen Robert Starkey, James L. Watkins, Lanny Lake, Raymond Mazza, Garry Lowther, and William Gregory; (eighth row) patrolmen Ronald Starkey, Michael Brown, Ira Hinkle, Antonio Romano, John Wilson, and Ronald Williams. (Courtesy of Clarksburg Police Department.)

91

A confiscated cache of marijuana and related paraphernalia are about to go up in smoke, as this photo in August 1974 would testify. From left to right are Lt. Gene Conaway, detectives Steve Toryak and Larry Robey, city manager Dick Barton (leaning over), narcotics agent Jim Hendrickson, finance director Donald Hoff, and chief of police Sam Paletta. (Courtesy of Clarksburg Police Department.)

Three slot machines that were confiscated from an undisclosed location in Clarksburg are about to be unloaded to face the sledgehammer in August 1974. At far right, holding the sledgehammer, is police chief Sam Paletta. The other gentleman is not identified. (Courtesy of Clarksburg Police Department.)

In 1901, these men were "Clarksburg's finest," members of the Clarksburg Police Department, with Mayor I.M. Kelly. Among the officers were police chief E.L. Stealey seated in front. Standing from left to right are T. Howe Light, R.N. Shields, H.E. Brooks (sic), W. Myers, J.J. Boggess, H. Lewis, J.L. Cunningham, George (sic) Crawford, A. Lyons, and Wade Huff. (Courtesy of Clarksburg Police Department.)

The White Electric Company is barely visible across the West Fork River during this flood in February 1957. The photo was taken from Hart Street in Stealey.

Both of these photos show the extent of the flood of 1957 in Clarksburg. In the above photo taken from Milford Street, lower Park Boulevard is seen under water from the raging West Fork River. Below, the water is very close to the bottom of the Stealey Bridge, on which traffic is backed up due to high water at the intersection of U.S. Routes 19 and 50 at West End. (Courtesy of Paul O. Hill.)

DAVIS-WEAVER FUNERAL HOME

AMBULANCE SERVICE

Phone 3500 Day or Night

CLARKSBURG, W. VA.

Time _10.30A_ Mileage _____ Date _June 6, 1948_

Name _____

Address _Marshville Rd._

For Ambulance
Service From _Residence_ $7.00

To _T.P._

Hospital _____ Room No. _____

Received Payment _____

By _Joe Hare_

Charge to _____

Address _____

Prior to the mid-1960s, ambulances from Clarksburg's funeral homes were called upon to assist especially when the city emergency cars were unavailable. This is a statement of services from the Davis-Weaver Funeral Home in June 1948 for an ambulance run to the Marshville Road west of the city. The bill came to a whopping $7. (Courtesy of James Murphy.)

The Union Protestant Hospital on lower Washington Avenue was a four-story structure where countless numbers of sick and injured people were treated. In about 1960, patients from the "U.P." were transferred to the new Union Protestant Hospital, off U.S. Route 19 South. That hospital, with several renovation and expansion projects and a merger with Saint Mary's Hospital, would become United Hospital Center, which stands at that location to this day. (Courtesy of Harrison County Medical Society.)

Here's an early image on a picture postcard of the Saint Mary's Hospital along Washington Avenue (then known as Mechanic Street). The closer building was formerly the Harrison County Hospital. Although the postcard does not indicate a date on the front, the postmark reveals an August 1910 dateline. (Courtesy of Paul O. Hill.)

96

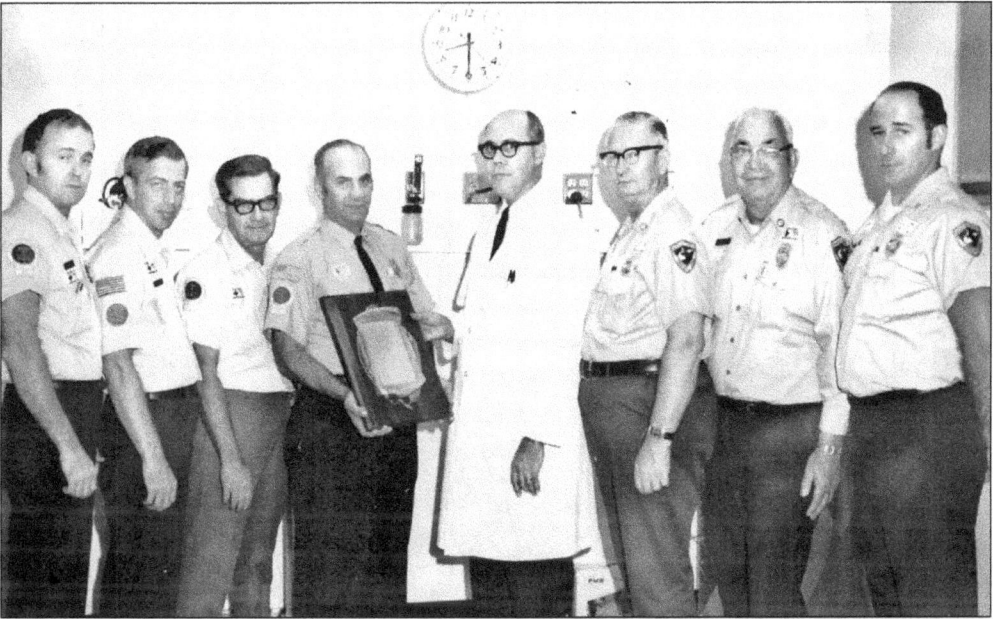

The Harrison County Emergency Squad was organized in 1966 as an all-volunteer group of emergency medical technicians. About 11 years later, paramedics were added and worked on a paying basis. Shown here in 1972, then-HCES president Louis "Zeke" Trupo presents a certificate to Dr. Burquess of the local V.A. Hospital "for his advice, help, cooperation and courtesy to the squad." From left to right are Charles Johnson, Walter Fultz, vice president Paul Ellison, Trupo, Burquess, Bernard Peck, "Pappy" Losh, and Jess Vasquez. (Courtesy of Fred Layman.)

The aerial truck of the Clarksburg Fire Department had to base itself on the lawn of the Point Comfort School on West Pike Street in the 1960s. The school was destroyed by the blaze. Perhaps ironically, it became the site of the West End station of the fire department. (Courtesy of Clarksburg Fire Department)

Construction on the Union National Bank was well under way in 1912, one year after one of the city's worst blazes destroyed the Trader's Hotel, which was located at that site. South Third Street was little more than a mud path in those days. (Courtesy of Dick Duez.)

Here's an old-fashioned hand-pumper behind the Clarksburg Fire Department's Central Station. The date is not known, but the Bridgeport Fire Department allegedly got the apparatus from Clarksburg. (Courtesy of Clarksburg Fire Department.)

The Monarch Pool Room in Clarksburg was razed by a fire on February 7, 1911. Note the icicles on the building toward the left of the image. (Courtesy of Dick Duez.)

The entire Clarksburg Fire Department was out in full "battle" array on Hewes Avenue in the early part of the 20th century, as this image shows. The building here would become the home of the *Exponent Telegram*, Clarksburg's daily newspaper. (Courtesy of Clarksburg Fire Department.)

This is a view of the Trader's Hotel sometime after firefighters brought the blaze that destroyed it under control, in early 1911. (Courtesy of Dick Duez.)

A highly destructive blaze in the early 1960s caused considerable damage to the West End Feed Company, the Check-R-Board dealer in Clarksburg. The building was located within inches of the B&O Railroad tracks in the city's West End. (Courtesy of Clarksburg Fire Department.)

Raw rubber burned for some time after fire caused extensive damage to the Empire Fabricating Company, located a short distance from the Veterans Hospital, on July 10,

1952. Residents in the area had to tolerate the odor for some time afterward. (Courtesy of Clarksburg Fire Department.)

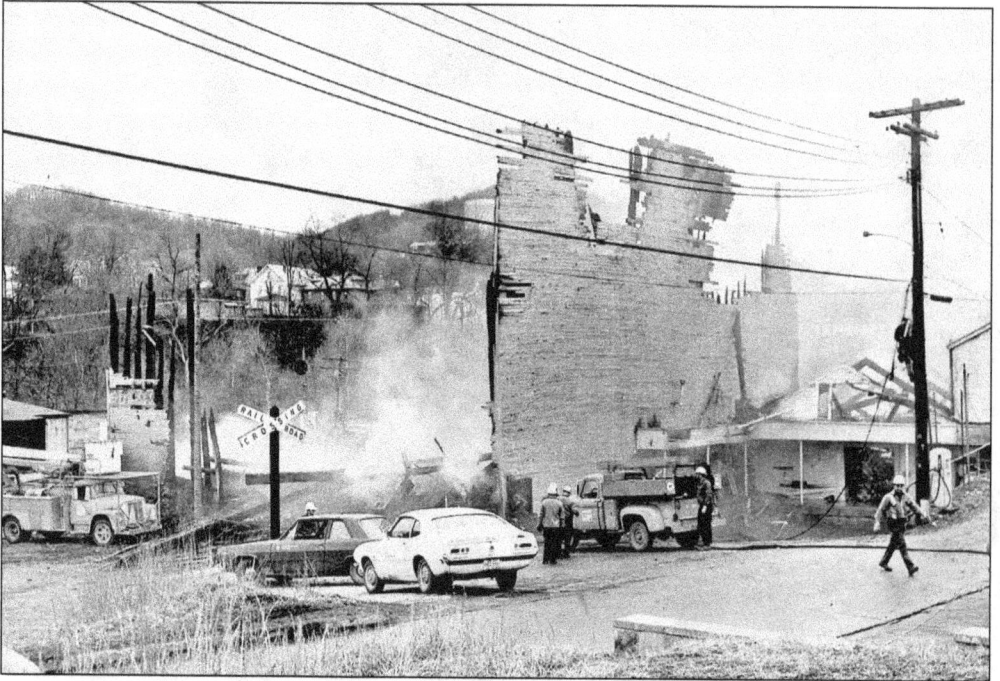

Not only were Clarksburg fighters called to battle this blaze just off Peck Street in the West End, but trucks from volunteer departments in several cities were called to assist. The blaze erupted on February 17, 1973. (Courtesy of Clarksburg Fire Department.)

These vehicles took quite a beating in the basement area of the Fuel City Metal Works on Ohio Avenue in Clarksburg's Montpelier Addition after fire caused much damage to the building on October 1, 1972. (Courtesy of Clarksburg Fire Department.)

Seven

WHERE WE LEARNED

These were the places where we would go—and still do—to learn life's lessons and how to solve the world's problems, large and small. Consolidation has decreased the actual number of schools in the Clarksburg area today, but the city boasted some of the better schools in the state in preceding generations. People who once attended the schools in Clarksburg have gone on to make positive strides in their own communities, in this country, or in the world. Also, churches of most denominations have existed in Clarksburg and have helped many people to learn how faith in God is the real key to their success. Photos of some of these places of learning in the Clarksburg area follow.

Washington Irving High School is shown here in 1961. Located on Lee Avenue, W.I. was a four-year school until 1990, when it consisted of just sophomores, juniors, and seniors; students attending the school transferred to the new Robert C. Byrd High School two miles away after the fall semester in 1995. The Hilltoppers were a force to be reckoned with in athletics, as well as academics.

Notre Dame High School on East Pike Street was brand new in 1956, and students who had attended Saint Mary's High School began taking their classes next door at N.D.H.S. Like the university of the same name, Notre Dame High chose the nickname "the Fighting Irish" for its athletic teams.

Clarksburg's Victory High School, shown here, was located on West Pike Street in the city's Adamston section for many years. The Eagles of Victory were also formidable opponents for whatever teams faced them in athletic activities. Also a good high school, students there began attending the new Liberty High School in 1973. The building above now houses Adamston Grade School.

Kelly Miller High School is where African-American students took classes until it graduated its final senior class in 1955. Its legendary principal was E.B. Saunders. The school stood on Water Street. The building today houses the Harrison County Schools system. A few years ago, the City of Clarksburg renamed Water Street, changing it to E.B. Saunders Way.

Liberty High School, located on Davisson Run Road (West Virginia Route 98), is shown from the air in this photo taken in the late 1970s. Liberty opened in 1973, and its Mountaineers are prominent in football, basketball, and baseball, as well as other sports. A new middle school, to be a "feeder" school for Liberty, has been planned nearby.

Students of the Clarksburg Graded School appear in this April 1890 photo. C. Lynch was the principal of the school. The list of students included Daisy Whitwain, Stella Devaughn, Bell Pinnell, Ida Sherwood, Daisy Orr, Edna Lepley, Grace Kennedy, Annie Meathrell, Cecelia Hurst, Beryl Stealey, Nellie Lang, Bertha Smith, Beulah Morgan, Eva Pike, Pearl Stealey, Rose Crim, Mary Kester, Jennie Harrison, Icie Smith, Mattie Morris, Georgie Bell, Nellie Williams, Tuny McCarty, Esther Riley, Charlie Craig, Willie Everson, Charlie Green, Fred Jackson, Richard Goodwin, and Charlie Griffin. Others named were J.G. Gittings and Fannie S. Rapp. (Courtesy of the Harrison County Historical Society.)

The First Methodist Church kindergartners enjoyed a Christmas party, complete with Santa Claus, in December 1952. Teachers were Mrs. Henry Mayer and Mrs. Charles Mayer. Some of the members included John McCuskey, Benjamin Cooksey, Ernest Gimmel, Edward Bynum, Mary Lou Sachs, and Caroline Hornor. (Courtesy of Mary Lou Sachs Hall.)

One of the two sixth grade classes at Morgan Elementary School in Stealey is shown with the teacher, Lois Rimmer. Philip N. Sheets was principal of the school when this photo was taken in October 1956. The school was demolished in the 1990s after students transferred to the newly-expanded Nutter Fort School. (Courtesy of Carolyn Smith.)

Sixth graders at Pierpont Grade School in Clarksburg during the 1958–1959 school year appear in this photo. Miss Alice Whelan was their teacher. From left to right are (front row) Gary Law, Kent Thrush, Dan Ayers, Frank Martino, David Cobb, Jerry Darquenne, Larry Burton, and Charles Fuller; (middle row) Pam McWilliams, Sandra Harrison, Randi Williams, Lana Myers, Joyce Morrison, Alexis San Julian, Joyce ?, Sandra Wade, Cathy Ross, Gloria Abruzzino, and Pam ?; (back row) Larry Davis, Steve King, Larry Wilson, Ernest Fragale, Sandra Basnett, Carolyn Sheets, Irene Connor, Linda Newport, Mary Lou Sachs, Lynn Montgomery, James Ali, and Bob Aaron. (Courtesy of Mary Lou Sachs Hall.)

The Saint Mary's School of Nursing was housed in this old familiar brick building in the 600 block of West Main Street in Clarksburg, a very short walk from Saint Mary's Hospital. DeSales Hall, as it came to be known, would later have physicians' offices there. It was eventually demolished, the site became a parking lot for several years, and subsequently the new Gaston Caperton Center of Fairmont State College (now University) was built there.

Adamston Grade School appears in this photo taken from West Pike Street at the corner of South Twenty-third Street. The old Victory High School is the home of Adamston Grade School today. (Courtesy of Pauline LeRoy.)

This is Christ Episcopal Church, perhaps the oldest church in Clarksburg and one of the oldest in Harrison County. It has been located on West Main Street at the corner of Sixth Street for scores of years.

Saint Paul's Methodist Church faced South Chestnut Street at West Main through the first five decades of the 20th century. The house at right was razed when the church closed. The main building now houses the Seventh Day Adventist Church.

The Clarksburg Baptist Church, at the corner of West Pike and Sixth Streets in Clarksburg, has been a mainstay in the city for many a decade. With several renovations and the addition years later of its Judson Center, it looks quite different today. (Courtesy of the Harrison County Historical Society.)

The Stealey Heights Methodist Church appears in this photo taken in 1961. The education building at right had been added in later years. It is now known as the Stealey United Methodist Church.

The First Presbyterian Church is a landmark at West Main and South Second Streets in downtown Clarksburg. The church's Westminster Hall is at left. The cornerstone for the church building was laid on September 27, 1893, and the church was dedicated on June 17, 1894.

When this photo was taken in probably the late 1940s, it was known as the South Chestnut Street E.U.B. Church. In 1968, it became the South Chestnut Street United Methodist Church. It stands at the corner of South Chestnut and Arthur Avenue in Chestnut Hills. (Courtesy of Robert L. Van Horn.)

These are some of the students and teachers at the Adamston School, shown at approximately the turn of the 20th century. No one is identified. (Courtesy of Dick Duez.)

The spire of the First Methodist Church towers over this part of downtown Clarksburg. The church was built in 1952 at the corner of West Pike and North Second Streets. It replaced the old First Methodist Church, which was destroyed by fire in September 1951. It is now the First United Methodist Church. In the foreground is Matthews Mobil service station and parking.

The Victory Eagles High School Band, shown here, was one of the best scholastic bands in central West Virginia in the 20th century. Victory High's colors were orange and black. This photo was taken in about 1952. (Courtesy of James A. Murphy.)

The Central Church of Christ, which was new when this photo was taken in the early 1960s, is on South Chestnut Street at the corner of Washington Avenue near downtown Clarksburg.

The Immaculate Conception Catholic Church of Clarksburg stands next to Notre Dame High School on East Pike Street.

CARLILE (Grades 1-6)

Carlile Grade School, which was on Maple Street in Clarksburg, appears in this photo. Students in grades one through six attended the school. (Courtesy of Pauline LeRoy.)

Eight

THEY ENTERTAINED US

There were the places that we'd go to see a movie, either an indoor cinema or a drive-in movie. There were places people could go to see a good play. There have long been opportunities for sports fans to attend baseball, football, or basketball games, or to enjoy a more active role, such as playing golf, tennis, or going bowling. These are but a few pastimes that have interested people for years—yes, and right in or around the Clarksburg area. A few of the places to go are featured in the remaining pages of this work, which also show some of the participants on various athletic teams in the Clarksburg area.

This is the front of the Ritz Theater on West Pike Street in Clarksburg. The ticket price in 1958, when this photo was taken, was $1.25 for adults and 21¢ for children. In the late 1950s, City Lines bus drivers would often get change from the Ritz Newsstand next door. (Courtesy of James A. Murphy.)

The Ellis Drive-in Theater and Restaurant had become a favorite of Clarksburg residents through the years. It was located along U.S. Route 50 between Clarksburg and Bridgeport. Neither the drive-in nor the restaurant exists today. (Courtesy of Ronnie Smith.)

The Skyline Drive-in Theater was another popular place to go and was only three miles out of town along U.S. Route 19 South.

A re-enactment of United States Marines raising the American flag on Iwo Jima Island near the end of World War II took place during the Veterans Day Parade, which is always a big event in Clarksburg. The men in the image were part of the 98th Infantry Division of the United States Marine Reserves. At left is Claude Gibbs Sr. The others were not identified. (Courtesy of Brenda Bonnell.)

A large parade featuring numerous bands from central West Virginia was held on the first Saturday of May each year as part of the North Central West Virginia Area Band Festival.

The annual Christmas parade was also a favorite of Clarksburg residents each year. The Morgan School P.T.A. built this float of Santa and his reindeer, captured in a November 1962 photo.

These majorettes lead one of the bands down West Main Street in this image from the early 1960s. The parade was discontinued in later years.

A quite prominent band director in Clarksburg was Henry "Hank" Mayer, shown leading the Washington Irving High School Hilltoppers Band along West Main Street in front of the McCrory's and G.C. Murphy's dime stores.

Here is a scene from the "Marching Club" Elks Convention in Clarksburg in 1922. This is looking

A shelter and picnic table at River Bend Park in Clarksburg had no users on this summer day in 1961. Many a picnic has been held at the park, now known as the Veterans Memorial Park. A playground area is also located at the park today.

west at the foot of West Main Street. (Courtesy of the Harrison County Historical Society.)

"Up a Lazy River" might be an appropriate theme song for this image, taken near the River Bend Park in 1961. The West Fork River has been a favorite place for fishermen over the years.

Football team members of the old Clarksburg High School appear in the 1903 images both above and below. The gentleman with the moustache in the bottom photo is Orie McConkey, who later became principal of Washington Irving High School, a post he held for more than 40 years. (Courtesy of Dick Duez.)

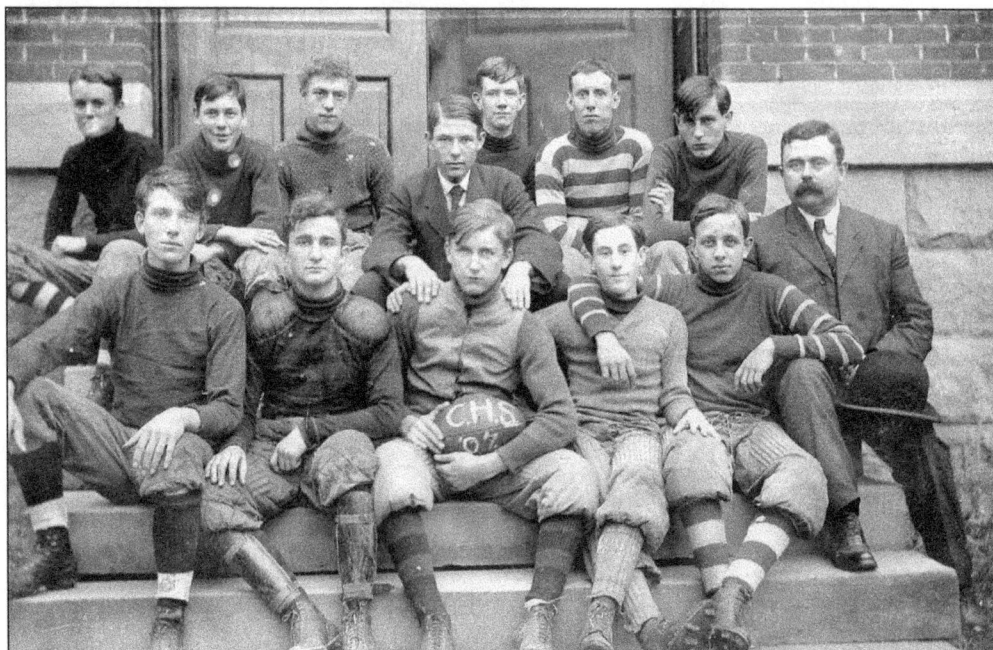

Harness races, as shown here, and horse races were held regularly during the annual Clarksburg Fair, which took place in Highland Park, now a part of the Stealey section of Clarksburg. Highland Park was located off lower Milford Street where Park Boulevard is today. (Courtesy of the Harrison County Historical Society.)

Compton Bowling Lanes, located along Bridgeport Hill Road (old U.S. Route 50), has for years been the only place for bowling enthusiasts to ply their expertise in the Clarksburg area. Another bowling center, Jewel City, went out of business about 25 years ago.

Far too many motion pictures and stage performances to recall them all have been seen at the Robinson Grand Theater in Clarksburg, the seating for which is seen here. The building still stands on West Pike Street, but the theater, which later became known as the Rose Garden, is virtually unused today. (Courtesy of Dick Duez.)

The second floor of the W.P. Holden Building, on the southwest corner of Third Street and Traders Avenue, housed an opera house and theater in the late 19th century. In May 1886 was the first performance by the Clarksburg Concert Company in the Music Hall, pictured here. Among those in the photo are Mannie Haymond Jarvis, Hal Rapp, Lou Patton, Frank Moore, and Carrie Bassel. No further identification was provided. (Courtesy of Harrison County Historical Society.)

The 13-year-old Babe Ruth League state champions in 1966 were from Clarksburg, having won the state title in Saint Albans, near Charleston. Coaches were Tom Fluharty and Bill Nolan. The late Pete Romano, at right, was long-time commissioner of the Harrison County Babe Ruth League. (Courtesy of Ruth Lawrence Bellotte.)

In the late 1940s, the Secret's Furniture Babe Ruth League team was a formidable foe for teams that it faced. From left to right are (front row) coach Pat Secret, Richard Frame, unidentified batboy, and Jim Daugherty; (middle row) unidentified player, Frank Secreto, John Oliveto, Joe Mancina, F. Merandi, Warren Spellman, and Sam Bellotte; (back row) unidentified player, E. Merandi, Pat Oliveto, unidentified player, Jack Privlege, "Skeeter" Bell, and Pete Perri. (Courtesy of Ruth Lawrence Bellotte.)

The Elks Little League baseball team of 1964 is shown here. From left to right are (front row) John Michael Mazza, Bill Pulice, Danny Hannah, Bob Thomas, Fred Arbonnaise, Junior McQuain, Clifford Fox, and John Maditz; (middle row) Russell Amos, Gary Lee Kennedy, unidentified player, John Jenks, Dana Maditz, Ralph Thomas, and Robbie Felton; (back row) manager George Feenie McQuain, assistant coaches Daniel E. Stalnaker and Frank Young, and assistants to manager Chuck Paugh and Jim Kennedy. (Courtesy of Bonnie Stalnaker.)

www.ingramcontent.com/pod-product-compliance
Lightning Source LLC
Chambersburg PA
CBHW080612110426
42813CB00006B/1486